THE

21

IMMUTABLE
LAWS
of
RELATIONSHIPS

FOLLOW THEM, WIN FRIENDS,
LEAD WELL AND INFLUENCE PEOPLE

GREGORY LAN IJIWOLA, PH.D.

Summit House
Publishers
Chicago, IL

The 21 Immutable Laws of Relationships
Copyright © 2017 by Gregory Lan Ijiwola, PH.D.

Paperback ISBN 978-0-9746735-5-4

Printed in the United States of America

Cover Design & Layout by Rotimi Kehinde

DEDICATION

To my dear father-in-law, Dr. A.A Ashaye. I know of few who have mastered the art of empowering relationships as you do. You practice these laws all the time with everyone. Observing you all these years has taught me some of the greatest lessons in people skills that I have learned.

CONTENTS

Acknowledgments | *vii*

Introduction | *ix*

PART 1..**11**

Chapter One | The Law of Non-Isolation:

Life must be shared. Your purpose on earth cannot be fulfilled in isolation....................13

Chapter Two | The Law of Partnership:

Relationships will multiply your efforts several fold. Great relationships

add pleasantness and power to your life..21

Chapter Three | The Law of Impartation:

You will become like those you closely associate with. So, choose wisely........................29

Chapter Four | The Law of The Measure:

Your ability to relate with people lovingly is a witness to and a measure of your

spirituality. Relationships are trainers and tests of character..37

Chapter Five | The Law of New Seasons:

It is through relationships that God opens you up into new seasons of life or new

territories in the pursuit of your divine purpose..41

PART 2..**47**

Chapter Six | The Law of Orchestration:

God will arranges divine relationships for you if you trust him to do so........................49

Chapter Seven | The Law of Intentionality:

Acquaintances may be accidental but relationships are made and built deliberately.

Intentionality may require your repositioning..55

Chapter Eight | The Law of Conversion:

God-sent people often come as strangers or enemies. Learn the process of conversion.......61

Chapter Nine | The Law of Blanketing:

Treat everyone honorably because you don't know which one is an angel

& all deserve honor...69

Chapter Ten | The Law of The Circles:

There are levels of relationships and not everyone is at the same level with you.

The choice of who occupies your innermost circles is yours to make.

Relationships should never be forced on you..73

PART 3..**79**

Chapter Eleven | The Law of Priorities:

The quality of your horizontal relationships is influenced by your vertical

relationship...81

Chapter Twelve | The Law of The Goose:

Relationships thrive and yield long-term benefits when fed and nurtured,

but die when exploited for instant or selfish gratifications.....................................87

Chapter Thirteen | The Law of Reciprocity:

Give into relationships what you want from it. You will reap

what you sow somewhere, sometime...91

Chapter Fourteen | The Law of The Center:

The world doesn't revolve around you. Earth's population with one exception

consists of others. To have fulfilling relationships, the center must shift away

from you to others...97

Chapter Fifteen | The Law of The Lifeblood:

Communication is the life-blood of every relationship. It must keep flowing.

Without it, relationships wane and die.................................105

Chapter Sixteen | The Law of Proactivity:

Don't let the actions of others dictate your REACTIONS.

Let principles and values dictate your ACTIONS.........................115

Chapter Seventeen | The Law of The Log:

Others aren't the initial problems to fix in your relationships, you are.

Positive changes in relationships come by focusing on changing the person

in the mirror first...121

Chapter Eighteen | The Law of The Rock:

Trust is the rock upon which all great relationships are built.

If trust is broken, there is nothing left to build on...............127

Chapter Nineteen | The Law of Expectations:

Believing the best of people brings out the best in people or at least it keeps

you sane. Trust people until they give you enough reasons no to.

Even then, find an excuse for them if you can........................137

Chapter Twenty | The Law of The Cover:

Faulty relationships do not have to be dysfunctional. Relationships that will

work should not give attention to every fault, but let love cover many faults..................143

Chapter Twenty One | The Law of The Fence:

Relationships need boundaries to thrive. Establish them. Make war to make peace.

Confront unresolved issues within yourself and in your relationships with the aim

of achieving harmony, then move on...151

ACKNOWLEDGMENTS

Writing a book is a team effort. I appreciate everyone who contributed in one way or the other to make this book a reality.

Many thanks to Ella Lameyer and Peace Udechukwu for your help and encouragement in getting the manuscript completed.

Special thanks to my moms, Beatrice Ijiwola and Josephine Ashaye for their prevailing prayers and support. I really needed it throughout the process.

I am ever grateful to my wife, Debo, for always standing by me and spurring me on. Thanks to my children: Jesse, Joshua and Pearl, who graciously allowed "Daddy" to have uninterrupted time to focus on writing and kept on checking to see if I was done.

INTRODUCTION

Everyone is in a relationship with someone. The question is not if you will have relationships. It is whether your relationships will be successful and beneficial to you, those involved with you, and others. The answer to this question is what this book is about.

A relationship is the way two or more people are connected together, behave toward, and deal with one another. We are born into relationships. From our time in the womb, we develop a relationship with our mothers. We are born, and we are involuntarily thrust into other relationships with our father, siblings, and extended families. We grow up and enter other relationships by choice: friends, coworkers, spouses, neighbors, and others. These relationships affect us, mold us, and make or break us, depending on their individual dynamics. We laugh in some, we cry in others. We reminisce about some and regret others. Some leave empowering imprints, others destructive marks. We all know relationships can be good or detrimental. But what makes them work? Are there certain principles and laws undergirding successful relations? If there are, what are they?

I have always been fascinated by the subject of relationships. From childhood, I found the observation of human relations intriguing. I mused many times on the dynamics of relationships: Why do people like or hate to be with others? Why are some happy while they are together and others are sad? Why do some work together amicably while others can't so much as see eye to eye? What makes some relationships work and others fail? Why are relationships even necessary? Is there some organized scheme behind the subject of human relations that one could learn in order to be good in living and working with others?

I first realized that human relations had some principles that one could employ to make them work better when I came across the popular book, How To Win Friends and Influence People by Dale Carnegie as a 4th grade student. I remember reading the book and internalizing the principles taught in the book. Reading it marked the beginning of my quest to uncover the principles that govern relationships.

My life journey so far also contributed to this quest. I grew up in Lagos, Nigeria, but now I live in Chicago and I travel to different nations in my work as a pastor, missionary author, and leadership consultant. This has exposed me to all kinds of relationships. I am blessed with acquaintances, friendships, and partnerships across geographical, economic, and ethnic boundaries internationally.

I have discovered from observation that there are certain universal principles of relationships that hold no matter where one is. We all have the same needs and wants and we respond to similar relational stimuli irrespective of our locations. I came to see that human relationships were not without underlying laws. They obeyed certain universal principles, which when applied, created successful relationships. This is true because human nature is the same universally. Understanding and practicing these principles proficiently is often referred to as possessing "people skills".

This was concretized in me reading the Bible. While scanning through the Scripture and meditating on passages dealing with human relations, the principles of relationships shared in this book coalesced. What I observed from immersion experiences in various relational settings came together into these principles.

This book is a summary of what I have learned so far. I hope it is a blessing to you. I pray it enriches your relation-"ships"—the ships we all sail into the fulfillment of God's plan for our lives. I begin with principles that focus on the successful initiation of relationships, then turn to the topic of nurturing and harnessing relationships. I have practiced these principles in my life, and they have been attested to by the many fruitful relationships across the globe that are changing the lives of millions. I have come to see that initiating, nurturing, and mobilizing relationships for world changing causes is what fulfilled living looks like. I believe if you learn these principles, internalize them, master them, and practice them, you will win friends, expand your network, develop more meaningful connections, lead well, and influence people. Let's get started!

Part
1

The first set of laws speak to the importance and benefits of relationships. Becoming aware of them and practicing them will give you tremendous motivation to maintain great relationships.

CHAPTER

1

THE
LAW
OF
NON-ISOLATION

*Life must be shared. Your purpose
on earth cannot be fulfilled in isolation.*

"Then the LORD God said, "It is not good for
the man to be alone…"" (Genesis 2:18)

Mankind was not created to live in isolation but in communities. You have probably read stories of individuals who were isolated for a period of time and the effects it had on them. A good one is the fictional story of Robinson Crusoe, who was shipwrecked and left on an island for several years.

In real life, one of the places isolation has showed its negative effects is in the prison system. Whenever prison officers want to punish inmates beyond incarceration for violating prison regulations, they put them in solitary confinement. The prisoner is isolated from human contacts for hours, days, weeks or even years. Although this action is often taken to either protect the prison population or the prisoner themselves from harm, it has been widely documented that the isolation produces extremely negative effects such as hallucinations, extreme anxiety, depression, loss of control, appetite loss and other mental, emotional, physical and social problems. The isolation compounds the problem. Man in any state was not created to be left alone.

The statement, "It is not good that the man be alone" has been interpreted by some to mean God decided Adam was lonely, so Eve was created to cure his loneliness. This is not what the verse means. Adam was *not* lonely. How could he be? He was in the presence of God. He had a purpose for living. He had his assignment from God and he was surrounded by the wonderful provisions of God. Loneliness is not the absence of companions, it is the absence of direction. It is possible to have lots of people surrounding you and in relationships with you, but still be lonely.

The statement implies God did not create you to fulfill your divine purpose in isolation. It is not saying you cannot be alone. Notice the statement was made in the context of assignment. You cannot fulfill your assignment in life alone. Every successful endeavor requires the cooperation of more than an individual. There is no self-made man. Every man is a product of others. You can't fulfill your assignment alone.

The Hebrew word used for "alone" here means to be "only himself" or to be "all one" meaning, it is not good for Adam to have all God has provided for him in creation and to carry out the assignment he received from God by himself alone. He needed someone like him to share the blessings and responsibilities— a helpmeet. God was saying in essence that He did not create man to function alone. Man was created for community. He was not to be a lone-ranger or recluse. Man can only reach the fullness of His potentials as he links up with other humans in partnership.

One cannot achieve significance. Relationships are needed for the fulfillment of destiny. It took another to teach you the alphabet, to take care of you as a helpless baby, to nurture you in childhood, and to lecture you in school. For the rest of your life, people will still have to play a significant role. In fact, there will come a time when you will become fully dependent on people again as you advance in age.

No success can be truly claimed by a person as his sole achievement. Every success builds on the works of others. Someone else planted the food you eat, assembled the car you drive, put together the tools you use. No man can be an island to himself. It is a law of God. Even if you struggle and achieve something, you can't enjoy it alone. Life was created to be shared, not hoarded. There is no lone-ranger in God's plans. Hermits are not his design.

A friend of mine shared the story of his late dad. While he was alive and younger and his kids were little, he mistreated them. He believed he did not need anyone, that he could survive on his own. Later, when he was older and his children were adults with their own families, he yearned for their presence and companionship, but no matter how the children tried, things did not connect. He lost the precious relationship he could have had with his children and grandchildren because he was ignorant of this principle earlier in life.

God is so smart, he made his creations to function maximally when they work together. His intention is not that his creation diverge. That is why he made everything dependent on something else. Look at the human body, no organ can function separately on its own. They are all interdependent. Any organ that becomes isolated will become diseased and will stop fulfilling its purpose. It dies.

Just like organs cannot exist on their own, you also cannot. Your vision in life will require partners. Every business needs other businesses and customers. Every church needs other churches. Every ministry needs other ministries. Even nations need other nations. Pastors need sheep to be pastors. Fathers need children. Even enemies need those they antagonize to earn their title. Even God, when he wanted to make man, said "Let us make man in our image." He didn't do it alone. He didn't create in isolation, but in cooperation. If you desire God's creative power in your life, you must also learn to synergize with others. You must learn to hook up with people, work with people, and be a team player.

The "us" concept is of God. The "I" concept is rooted in Satan. Remember what he said before he fell from his exalted position,

> "How you are fallen from heaven, O Lucifer, son of the morning! How you are cut down to the ground, You who weakened the nations! For you have said in your heart: 'I will ascend into heaven, I will exalt my throne above the stars of God; I will also sit on the mount of the congregation On the farthest sides of the north;I will ascend above the heights of the clouds, I will be like the Most High" (Isaiah 14:12-14)

Count the number of "Is" in his manifesto. There are five of them. Be careful when you begin to function using the "I" concept. When all you think about is yourself, your benefit, your space, your family, your business, or your vision, when life becomes all about you, you are operating in a spirit of isolation. Satan is cutting you off from others to destroy you. He wants to isolate you so he can insulate you.

Manifestations of Isolation

There are a couple of ways the spirit of isolation manifests itself. I will discuss them briefly here.

1. The Elitist Syndrome

This is the attitude that says "everyone is wrong but I am right, so I need to separate myself to avoid being contaminated by them." It is the spirit that says your own little club has it right while a large majority of others are wrong. It is a manifestation of pride. It is one of the primary identifying characteristics of a cult. Some churches suffer from this spirit and cannot listen to the teachings or tolerate the beliefs of other churches. If people don't do things the way they do it, it is wrong. Baptism must be according to their denomination's specifications. Anything that goes crosswise with their view is quickly labeled heretical and false. Individuals with such attitudes, in their pride, become more narrow-minded, hateful, and cut off from the benefit of learning from others.

2. The Sacrificial-Lamb Syndrome

I also call this the Elijah Syndrome. Those suffering from this syndrome believe they are the only ones who remain standing and suffering for a particular cause while others are only living in pleasure. They feel they are the only one left in the battle not knowing there are others fighting long with them from which they are only isolated. Elijah showed symptoms of this syndrome.

> "So it was, when Elijah heard it, that he wrapped his face in his mantle and went out and stood in the entrance of the cave. Suddenly a voice came to him, and said, "What are you doing here, Elijah?" And he said, "I have been very zealous for the Lord God of hosts; because the children of Israel have forsaken Your covenant, torn down Your altars, and killed Your prophets with the sword. I alone am left; and they seek to take my life." Then the Lord said to him: "Go, return on your way to the Wilderness of Damascus; and when you arrive, anoint Hazael as king over Syria...Yet I have reserved seven thousand in Israel, all whose knees have not bowed to Baal, and every mouth that has not kissed him." (I King 19:13-18).

You must let it sink into you that God is never left with you alone. Whatever God has told you to do, there are several others doing the same. You should try to link up with them. Don't get to a point where you feel you are the only one left. That is a deception of the enemy. It is a trick to isolate you.

3. The Wounded-Exile Syndrome

Individuals who suffer from this isolate themselves as a reaction to hurt or rejections they have faced from others. They might have tried to develop relationships and link up with others only to be rejected and hurt. As a result of this, they recoil into their shells and make up their minds not to be close to anyone again. They try to protect their heart from further hurt by shielding it through isolation. Unfortunately for them, in trying to protect themselves, they cut off other relationships essential for their success in life.

4. The Rat-Race Syndrome

This is as a result of a competitive spirit. People suffering from this isolate themselves because they approach life as a competition or race. Rather than simply seeking to excel, they focus on besting others. They see others as competitors rather than complementers. So, in order to maintain their supposed edge, they keep important secrets of their successes from others and limit access to them.

5. The Envy Syndrome

Those suffering from this deliberately isolate themselves because they cannot bear it to see others suffering or doing better than them. So, in order to insulate themselves from being confronted with the progress of others, they isolate themselves.

6. The Shame Syndrome.

Those suffering from this isolate themselves because of a perception that others will not like them if they knew them. This is usually a result of low self-esteem or habitual sin. They hide from others because they fear being discovered, exposed, or ridiculed.

7. The Rebellion Syndrome.

These isolate themselves because they do not want to be corrected, held accountable, or made to answer for the consequences of their actions.

8. The Lone-Ranger Syndrome

Lone rangers believe they can succeed on their own. They trust their abilities so much that they exclude others. For a variety of reasons, they resent company. It could be because they do not trust others or because they hope to singularly receive all the credit for the results. Some are lone rangers because of a highly introverted temperament. Whatever the motivation, being a lone ranger limits you. Focus is blind. When you are focused on one thing, there are many other things you miss. It takes the focus of others to see the full picture.

Consider Ecclesiastes 4:8-12,

"There is one alone, without companion: He has neither son nor brother. Yet there is no end to all his labors, Nor is his eye satisfied with riches. But he never asks, "For whom do I toil and deprive myself of good?" This also is vanity and a grave misfortune."
"Two are better than one, Because they have a good reward for their labor. For if they fall, one will lift up his companion. But woe to him who is alone when he falls, For he has no one to help him up." Again, if two lie down together, they will keep warm; But how can one be warm alone? Though one may be overpowered by another, two can withstand him. And a threefold cord is not quickly broken."

Lone rangers are underachievers. They accomplish less than their potential because they refuse to link up. They have no one to share in their successes. When they fall, there is no one to lift them up.

The Dangers of Isolation

From this passage in Ecclesiastes, you can also see that isolating yourself is dangerous. You are a cord that can easily be broken. Alone, you become more vulnerable to attack. Predators love sheep that are separated from the herd. A single strand is easily cut, but when it is weaved together with other strands, it becomes resilient. You also become stronger when you are in partnership with others and weaker when you isolate yourself.

Also, when you are isolated, you are insulated — cut off from the input of others. You are left to depend on your own ability and wisdom alone. But as you must know, that is a limited source. You need the wisdom, counsel, and input of others to succeed in your endeavors. An isolated person is left without enough resources to meet the challenges he or she faces. Your path in life becomes easier as you link up with others.

Are you a lone-ranger? Do you have the mistaken belief that you can go it alone in life or that you can be a "self-made" person? You weren't created to function like that. In your journey through life, you will need input from other individuals. You will need assistance from others no matter how gifted you are. Any idea or vision God has given you requires the partnership of others.

Dealing with Isolation

They key to dealing with isolation is to intentionally cultivate relationships. You must step out of your self-imposed exile. Repent of the elitist attitude. Fight the temptation to turn yourself into a sacrificial lamb. Don't let past wounds cause you to block off those that God sends your way to help you. Refuse to be a lone ranger by locating like-minded people that can partner with you in life. Deliberately go out of your way to join an authentic community where there is openness and vulnerability. Start connecting with the visions of other people. Always remember, this first principle of relationships is that success can never be achieved in isolation because significance always requires more than one. You will always need people. Now, let's look at the next law.

CHAPTER

2

THE
LAW
OF
PARTNERSHIP

Relationships will multiply your efforts several fold.
Great relationships add pleasantness and power to your life

"Two are better than one, because they have
a good reward for their labor..." (Ecclesiastes 4:9)

Scientists have observed that geese fly using a "V" pattern to make their flights easier. This formation allows each goose in flight to have an equal field of vision as the rest. A goose leads the formation, doing most of the work, but when it becomes tired, it moves to the back and another goose takes its place in front. This rotation continues on and on through their flight and conserves energy.

Another advantage of the V flight pattern is that, as each goose flaps its wings, it creates additional uplift for the bird immediately following. If one goose falls out of the formation, it immediately feels a drag that moves it to rejoin the group. Also, if one of the birds falls ill or gets shot and falls out of the formation, two other birds will follow it down to aid it until it either recovers or dies, and then rejoin the formation. The geese behind also honk to encourage the ones in front to keep the pace. This is just one example in nature of the power of partnership. We need partners to maximize life.

Two are better. To be better means to have good qualities to a greater degree than another. It means to be superior. Whatever is better is an enhanced and increased form of the other. So, two people are an enhancement of one. They operate on a greater degree than an individual. Relationships multiply individual efforts. What you can do alone, you can multiply by joining with others. There is an enhancement of result and strength when individuals come together with one focus.

Relationships are also protective. It is said that when a lion desires to catch its prey, it is harder when the prey is traveling in a pack. But when one wanders away from the pack, the lion easily pounces and kills the isolated prey. Being in relationships is like being in a pack, it is safer than being alone.

For example, if you are married, being with other couples, talking with them, and sharing your challenges, struggles, and joys, with other couples strengthens your marriage. If you are preparing for marriage, it will help you to get together with other engaged couples, praying and spending time together comparing notes. The same applies to those unattached. When you discover that others are going through exactly what you are, it makes you stronger.

One of the things that helps me the most as a pastor and leader is my relationships with other leaders. I deliberately seek other leaders and cultivate relationships with them. We have times we meet, share, and compare notes. In some of those meetings we find ourselves just laughing at ourselves. I go into some of the meetings feeling like I am the worst leader in the world and come out of it, after hearing the stories of others, that I wasn't that bad! I have accountability partners, men that cry together, laugh together, and join together to do greater things than we could have done on our own. There is just something empowering about linking up with others. Power and results are multiplied severalfold when you engage others in the things you do.

The Impossible Becomes Possible
Through Partnership

During the second World War, the United States led an effort tagged "The Manhattan Project" aimed at developing the first atomic bomb. The United Kingdom and Canada were also behind the effort. The goal of the project was to beat Hitler to the development of atomic weapons. It was an extensive project that required the contributions of scientists, engineers, and others. Over 130,000 people were employed working at over 30 sites at a cost of over $2 billion. It was an unprecedented project that required tens of thousands to work together, spurred by the common goal of defeating the Nazis. It was accomplished. The aftermath was the bombing of Hiroshima and Nagasaki, the end of World War II, and the beginning of a nuclear arms race that has left the possibility of the planet's annihilation to the decisions of a few individuals.

Another project that humans embarked upon, previously thought of as impossible, was the Apollo program. This was the effort of the United States to be the first to land a man on the moon and to accomplish it within a decade. It employed over 400,000 people and utilized the support of over 20,000 firms and universities at a cost of $24 billion dollars. Despite that this was the most complicated and hazardous journey humanity had ever embarked upon, spurred on by a unity of focus to achieve space superiority, it was accomplished in 1969, when Neil Armstrong became the first man to walk on the moon.

These two examples of human projects, among many accomplished by unity of focus and a strong motivation, are in line with God's statement in the following text about the man He created, that when united, whatever they set out to do will not be held back from them.

> "But when God came down to see the city and the tower mankind was making, 6 he said, "Look! If they are able to accomplish all this when they have just begun to exploit their linguistic and political unity, just think of what they will do later! Nothing will be unattainable for them! 7 Come, let us go down and give them different languages, so that they won't understand each other's words!" (Genesis 11:5-7 TLB)

Through unity and collaboration, humans can accomplish great feats. This is an ability God placed in man so man can carry out His purpose on the earth and for the whole of creation. It is part of the expression of the dominion God gave man at his creation.

In this passage of Genesis, God respected that ability. Now, though this is a God-given ability, the problem comes when man tries to use this ability for a purpose contrary to God's purpose or in rebellion to God, as the case was in our text.

They were united among themselves but not with God. When this takes place, the outcomes can be very disastrous. This is why God intervened to stop them. God was not afraid or jealous of what they could accomplish, He was concerned for them and the consequences of their accomplishment so He intervened to save man from himself.

There are many projects or endeavors you may find yourself drawn into in life. There are visions that will come into your heart or that others will share with you, asking for your participation and support, that may seem huge and impossible. Don't get scared at how daunting things may look. Your main concern is to find out if God is in the project, because if it is conceived in God, it is definitely achievable.

The Multiplied Reward of Partnership

When the influence of God is upon the relationship, the principle of agreement applies. One of my favorite passages, Deuteronomy 32:30, explains the principle of agreement.

"How could one chase a thousand," the passage asks, "and two put
ten thousand to flight, unless their Rock had sold them, and the
Lord had surrendered them?"

I love the progression in the passage.

It wasn't arithmetic but a geometric progression. If one chases a thousand, you would expect two to chase two thousand. But, rather, the passage says ten thousand. Because of God's involvement, the addition of one multiplied the result ten-fold. This is the principle of agreement at work. Jesus utilized this principle when he sent out his disciples two by two to the cities in very successful missions. The early church followed a similar pattern, displaying various combinations of ministry partners such as Paul and Silas and Paul and Barnabas.

Two by Two

"The Lord now chose seventy-two other disciples and sent them ahead in
pairs to all the towns and places he planned to visit." (Luke 10:1)

When Jesus sent out his disciples on missionary journeys, he sent them in pairs. This is a manifestation of divine wisdom. It is this wisdom that is also manifested in other expeditionary or ministry pairs we see throughout the Bible: Elijah and Elisha, David and Jonathan, Paul and Barnabas, Peter and John, Paul and Silas, Paul and Timothy, and many others. The story of Paul and Silas when they were jailed in Philippi illustrates the power of partnership (Acts 16).

Locked up in prison for preaching the gospel, with backs bleeding from flogging, they encouraged one another, praying and singing praises to God together. Peter and John, when confronted and flogged by the Sanhedrin, were emboldened together and later went to their companions and prayed together in literally a ground shaking way (Acts 4). Aaron and Moses had the same assignment, but different strengths. The combination of both in partnership became the terror of Pharaoh and Egypt, but the freedom of Israel from bondage. Partnership multiplies your strength.

> "But David said, "No, my brothers! The Lord has kept us safe and helped us defeat the enemy. 24 Do you think that anyone will listen to you when you talk like this? We share and share alike—those who go to battle and those who guard the equipment." (I Samuel 30:23-24 TLB)

This passage lays out a principle of partnership. When people join together in partnership, the task and associated weight are distributed so each partner does less than they would have done to achieve the same result if they were operating alone. Yet, the amazing thing is they get to share the reward equally. To illustrate, let's assume three people joined together in partnership for a project with a reward of $100. If one of the individuals did all the work alone, without partners and exerting much effort, he or she gets the $100. However, according to this principle, if the three individuals partner together to accomplish the same task, each will get $100 dollars even though the efforts exerted were lower than what they would have used alone.

Our church organizes an annual event called LightFest in Chicago. It is a community event where we share love with the community through acts of kindness. We set up a carnival-like atmosphere with inflatable jumps for kids, games for adults, food, and a free health check for all. When we first began organizing this event, we took on the full responsibility of putting it together. It was very costly, yet our results were minimal. A few years into organizing it, we partnered with another community organization, that also leveraged partnerships with other community organizations toward the event. We discovered that our cost was reduced but the result increased dramatically. Our partnership with these organizations reduced the strain on us and each organization in partnership, yet our joint result was multiplied. Each of us claimed in our reports that we accomplished the result. This is similar to each of us getting a $100 , when one alone would have gotten a lone $100.

There is a bettering and multiplying effect in doing life with others. You do more with others. Whatever you are doing, try to do it with someone. If you want to start an enterprise, find a co-founder. Find fellow visionaries you can join with. Don't go it alone. There is power in partnership. Pray to God to send you people that will stand and work in agreement with you. When people come together around any purpose, there is power to accomplish much, but when they come together around God's purpose and with God's backing, the power is multiplied and success is assured.

CHAPTER

3

THE
LAW
OF
IMPARTATION

You will become like those you closely associate with. So, choose wisely.

"Walk with the wise and become wise, for a companion of fools suffers harm..." (Proverbs 13:20)

Nature teaches us that when you place two objects of different temperatures together, the one with the higher temperature soon matches the colder one as it loses its heat. In the same way, you are becoming like those you closely associate with. The temperature of your life soon matches that of your closest friends. If they were hotter, you would gain some heat. If they are colder, you will lose your heat and reach their levels. This is the essence of the law of impartation.

People influence you. There is a subtle influence that goes on through relational interactions.

"When the Council saw the boldness of Peter and John and could see that they were obviously uneducated non-professionals, they were amazed and realized what being with Jesus had done for them!" (Acts 4:13 TLB)

The interaction of Peter and John with Jesus had changed them so much that they reflected his boldness and courage even when he was no longer physically with them, and people could see it. It covered their lack of education. The positive lesson in this is that you may have some personal deficit either in skill, wisdom, character, or otherwise, but if you begin to relate and interact with those who possess these characteristics, they will soon rub off on you and elevate you to a higher level.

In my book, *Irresistible Influence*, I enumerated five effects of association. I will repeat them here.

Five Effects of Association

1. Your Association Will Directly Influence your Character and Attitude

"He who walks with wise men will be wise, but the companion of fools will be destroyed." (Proverbs 13:20).

You can also increase your influence by carefully choosing the types of people with whom you associate. You become like those with whom you associate. As you interact closely with people, you increasingly become more like them. This is the law of association: there is an exchange and transfer of attitudes and characteristics by people who spend enough time together. Paul attests to this idea by writing, "Do not be deceived: "Evil company corrupts good habits" (1 Corinthians 15:33).

The old saying goes, "show me your friend and I'll tell you who you are". You will average out the characteristics of the people you associate with. This is the reason why good parents carefully monitor the types of friends their children keep and the places they frequent. They know that, given time, they would take on the characteristics of their friends.

"Don't hang out with angry people; don't keep company with hotheads. Bad temper is contagious— don't get infected." (Proverbs 22:24 MSG)

2. Your Association Affects your Environment

People have certain auras—particular atmospheres – surrounding them. When you associate with them closely for long enough, you share the same atmosphere. The spiritual and emotional environment around them diffuses into yours. Have you noticed your encounters with some individuals leave you sad, angry, or frustrated? You felt differently before your contact with them, but after your time with them, you sensed a totally different atmosphere around you. Your calm may have been disturbed. You may become more susceptible to temptations. You may have felt depressed. What happened is they transferred the aura around their lives to yours.

Conversely, there are other people who leave you inspired, joyful, and full of faith and hope. They leave you refreshed. These people have the right kind of atmosphere surrounding them. They are the kinds of people with whom you should spend most of your time.

Developing close relationships with them will allow you to consistently cloak yourself in their positive atmosphere. Saul met the prophets and began to prophecy (1 Samuel 10:11). The atmosphere of the prophets affected him. Do the people you move with have positive effects on you?

3. Association Will Either Increase, Diminish, or Multiply the God- Influence On You

In addition to affecting your atmosphere, your associations affect the level of God-influence flowing in your life. They will either block or enhance the flow. In his book, *Winning with People* John Maxwell wrote about four kinds of people that will come into our lives. The following is a brief description of them.

a. **Adders:** These are people who deposit good things into your life. They are good influences. They are usually good friends, confidants, and godly family members. You will recognize them by what happens to you in their presence. When you are with them, you feel inspired, loved, and believed in. They intentionally add value to your life and make your life more pleasant and enjoyable, increasing your capacity for influence. Celebrate these people.

b. **Subtractors:** This set of people takes from you unintentionally. Being with them puts a burden on you. They drain you of energy. They are receivers, not givers. You will recognize them by your response when they initiate contact with you. They are those you hesitate to answer phone calls from. Tolerate these people.

c. **Multipliers:** These are people who multiply your life. They greatly enhance you. They push you to be better. These are usually mentors and leaders. They push you into your potential. They are your coaches but not necessarily your friends. They will not tolerate your weaknesses; but will confront them. They love you and seek your increase. They multiply influence in your life. Value these people. Never take them for granted. Appreciate and celebrate them.

d. **Dividers:** These are people who cause strife and greatly diminish your life. They are different from subtractors because they are intentionally causing harm. Avoid such people. You need to identify those who occupy these categories in your life. Your response to each group should be different. Spend most of your time with adders and multipliers. Sometimes it may require some sacrifice to be with them. Pay the price. Sometimes your association with multipliers will be through their materials such as books and videos. Immerse yourself in them. The more you spend time with them, the sharper you become.

"As iron sharpens iron, so a man sharpens the countenance of his friend." (Proverbs 27:17)

Your cutting edge in life becomes more effective as you associate with adders and multipliers.

On the other hand, try to limit your interaction with subtractors and dividers. Tolerate the subtractors but, if possible, avoid the dividers. It is also important that you do not *become* a subtractor or divider. Work to be a multiplier or adder to other people. Seek to give in relationships not simply to get.

4. Association Will Either Limit or Enlarge your Vision

The following story illustrates the power associations can have to limit potentials.

There was an eaglet that fell from the safety of its nest while it was young. A farmer found the young eaglet and took it to his farm. He raised the eaglet in a chicken coop among his many chickens. As the eagle grew up, it began to act like the chickens around it. It ate what the chickens ate and did everything the chickens did. Though it was a very powerful eagle that could soar in the sky, it was grounded and did not fly.

One day, a man came to the farm and saw the eagle acting like a chicken. He immediately recognized the problem. The man decided to help this eagle discover itself. He separated it from the chickens and took it to a very tall part of the farmhouse, but the eagle still could not fly. Later the man took the eagle far away to a high mountain where they could no longer see the farm house. Other eagles soared in the mountain. The man released the eagle and soon it was flapping its wing and flying. As long as they were close to the chicken coop, the eagle could not fly. It took a dramatic change of company from chickens to fellow eagles before the eagle could unleash its potential.

Change Your Company

Like this eaglet, you may need to change your company if the law of impartation is working against you. If you are surrounded by chickens, there are two things that have to change. You have to leave the coop and you have to leave the company of chickens. You were created to fly in unrestricted skies.

Lot, Abraham's nephew's, life also demonstrates how associations can limit your potential. When God told Abraham to leave his father's house to a land God would show him, without any instruction from God, Lot attached himself to Abraham and left with him. Lot soon began to enjoy the same blessings Abraham received. Lot became very wealthy as a result of his association with Abraham. Later, he made a mistake and separated from Abraham. When Lot moved close to Sodom and Gomorrah, he was exposed to the lifestyle of the land. This move almost cost him everything. Association matters.

5. Your Association Affects your Reach

Frigyes Karinthy came up with the "Six Degrees of Separation" concept which proposes a human web in which each person is linked to any other person in the world by, at most, approximately six people. This idea speaks to reach, the number of people to whom you are connected. Influence works through reach. Association multiplies your reach. As you associate, you jump from degree to degree towards people that need your influence. Every individual you see has a certain circle and will expand that circle. Therefore, your association of influence with that individual will extend your influence beyond your own current circle with unlimited possibilities. I have seen this concept at work in my life. As I develop relationships with certain individuals, I suddenly find myself influencing their circles. I have seen families influenced through my association with just one member of the family. I have seen churches and other institutions influenced through my life as a result of my association with certain individuals who have access to those places.

Always be conscious of the fact that every individual you see has a certain circle and will continue to expand that circle. Your association of influence with that individual will extend your influence beyond your own current circle with unlimited possibilities.

Bill Bright's ministry, Campus Crusade for Christ, also demonstrates this principle. This ministry was founded in 1951 at the University of California, Los Angeles in order to impact future leaders. From their initial relationships with University of California college students, the organization's influence has grown to reach more than 190 countries around the world, employing over 25,000 full-time missionaries, and has trained over 225,000 volunteers around the world. This ministry's initial reach of college students extended through the ever growing associations of students to reach its current network. This is an amazing example of multiplying influence into ever increasing circles by means of relationships.

As you make friends, be aware that your associations will influence you. Have influence on your mind as you contemplate linking up and getting closer to people.

CHAPTER

4

THE
LAW
OF THE
MEASURE

*Your ability to relate with people lovingly is a witness
to and a measure of your spirituality.
Relationships are trainers and tests of character.*

"This is how everyone will recognize that
you are my disciples—when they see the love
you have for each other." (John 13:35 MSG)

Measurements play an important role in life. From basic daily tasks such as getting the right amount of ingredients mixed together for cooking or taking the temperature of your child with a thermometer, checking your weight on the bathroom scale, or checking what time of day it is, to more complex uses such as finding the areas and volumes of different materials.

Measurements are used in all professions. Airplane pilots rely on precise measurements of elements such as air pressure and temperature, speed, altitudes, and so on to safely convey people from place to place. Nurses and doctors measure out doses of medications and check the vitals of people to do their work. Engineers and architects read blueprints with definite dimensions and markings.

In physics, if you wanted to measure a physical phenomenon, you often cannot measure it directly. However, by measuring its effect on another object, you can obtain a reliable approximation of its quantity or quality. For example, to measure the temperature of an object, you quantify its expanding or contracting effects on mercury in a thermometer and thus obtain its measure. Similarly, if you want to know how healthy a person is, you measure their vitals. You check pulse rate, heart rhythm, blood pressure, weight, and height for their body-mass index, cholesterol level, and so on. The data obtained from this reveals their state of health. It is a witness to the important but intangible quality — their health.

The Witness Law of relationship is analogous to this. To know the quality of an invisible intangible, like loving an invisible God, one would have to measure a visible effect of it — your practice of love with people.

> "If anyone says "I love God," but keeps on hating his brother, he is a liar; for if he doesn't love his brother who is right there in front of him, how can he love God whom he has never seen?" (I John 4:20)

If you wanted to truly know the measure of your relationship with God, the gauge is your relationship with people. The quality of your horizontal relationships with people is a witness to the quality of your vertical relationship with God. How you relate with people attests to your character and spirituality.

If you cannot stand people, your relationship with God is questionable. God lives in people and loves people. The true measure of your spirituality is your ability to relate with God's people. You know the level of your love by how it is expressed to people you least like.

God is a people person. His desire has always been to build a kingdom, a family, an army of people. So walking with God necessitates loving people or you will not enjoy or endure in his presence and purpose. The pursuit and development of godly relationships is, therefore, an essential part of your relationship with God. You must learn to walk with people. How you are able to do this is a pointer to the quality of your closeness to God.

According to the John 13:35, the recognition of your discipleship is the love you have learned to show. Discipleship is not attested to by church attendance, the size of your bible, or the amount of scriptures you are able to rattle out per second, but by love. Love is the ability to treat people like God treats you and them.

Applying the Law of the Witness

So how do you apply this law in your relationships? Realize that whatever can be measured can be improved. Accountability leads to growth. Metrics lead to profitability.

> "Any enterprise is built by wise planning, becomes strong through common sense, and profits wonderfully by keeping abreast of the facts."
> (Proverbs 24:3 TLB)

This law helps you keep abreast of the vitality of your relationship with God so you can make continual adjustments and improvements. Always be watchful of how you see, talk about, and relate with the people God brings into your life. If you treat them with love, you are growing in your relationship with God. If you find it hard to get along and are always irritated with them, be sincere with yourself. Let this be a pointer to you of the need to grow more in your walk with God. So this law is not only a thermometer for measuring the temperature of your walk with God, but also a thermostat for spurring you on to higher levels of spiritual growth and, consequently, better relationships with the people in your life.

CHAPTER
5

THE
LAW
OF
NEW SEASONS

It is through relationships that God opens you up into new seasons of life or new territories in the pursuit of your divine purpose.

"Then Barnabas brought him to the apostles and told them how Paul had seen the Lord on the way to Damascus, what the Lord had said to him..." (John 13:35)

Chicago has been appropriately nicknamed the windy city and I have often heard it said by many who live here that Chicago has mostly every other thing but good weather. As I write this, just some few days earlier, cars plowed through mountains of snow. Streets were deserted of walking pedestrians.

Everyone was clad in heavy overcoats and multiple layers of clothing within their vehicles. Trees hung still in deathlike postures and the birds reserved their songs.

Winter can be a messy season. Long lines of traffic on Interstate 90. Snow trucks fighting losing battles. Messy sidewalks and driveways. Skidding cars. Restless kids converting the desire for outdoor adventures into mischief around the house. Depressed granddads and moms. Winter could also be economically demanding. Escalated energy bills. A fresh consignment of winter wear for the kids.

This morning was different, though. I stepped outside and, instead of the cold and chilly, a refreshing wind greeted my face. Spring had come.

Soon the flowers will blossom again. The green of the grasses will replace the once dry and yellow carpets of lawns and meadows. Rain will fall again and everything will spring forth. The birds will take up their songs again as every last bit of ice melts beneath radiant sunshine.

Soon, men and women will leave the confines of winter and frolic on the streets again. Pools, lakes, parks, and beaches will once again teem with people basking in the fun of a new season. I can't help but think of life in such a poetic moment. Life's seasons do change. A new season brings new realities.

You may be in the winter of life right now. The very atmosphere around you is chilly and messy. The bill compartment is bulging with unpaid bills. You slipped at work and got the pink slip. Depression hangs around you and you seem to have lost your song. Are you bereaved or abandoned? Dreams of changing the world fading in the face of debts and bills? Hold on hope because a new season will come and one of the ways God does this is to bring new relationships into your life.

Life advances in seasons and, when God wants to move you into a new season of life, he will use relationships around you to facilitate it, usually new relationships. When the devil wants to do the same, he uses similar method. This is why you always have to properly evaluate new relationships because every relationship you pursue will usher you into a new season of life.

How does God bring us into new seasons of life? He does this by opening us up to new revelations, fresh information, or a new circle of relationships. Relationships are the "ships" we ride into new horizons in our journeys of purpose in life. New relationships will help make or mar you, keep you focused and advancing, or they will distract and derail you.

Paul, the apostle, benefited greatly from this principle. In our text, Barnabas was used by God to introduce Paul to the other apostles. That introduction marked the beginning of a new season in Paul's life. Earlier on, God had used another new relationship with Ananias to clarify Paul's call.

> "Now there was in Damascus a believer named Ananias. The Lord spoke to him in a vision, calling, "Ananias!" "Yes, Lord!" He replied. 11 And the Lord said, "Go over to Straight Street and find the house of a man named Judas and ask there for Paul of Tarsus. He is praying to me right now, for 12 I have shown him a vision of a man named Ananias coming in and laying his hands on him so that he can see again!"... So Ananias went over and found Paul and laid his hands on him and said, "Brother Paul, the Lord Jesus, who appeared to you on the road, has sent me so that you may be filled with the Holy Spirit and get your sight back." 18 Instantly (it was as though scales fell from his eyes) Paul could see and was immediately baptized. 19 Then he ate and was strengthened. He stayed with the believers in Damascus for a few days 20 and went at once to the synagogue to tell everyone there the Good News about Jesus— that he is indeed the Son of God!" (Acts 9:10-19 TLB)

Later on in Paul's ministry, God also used relationships to usher him into a new season of apostolic mission when he and Barnabas were commissioned by some other friends.

> "Among the prophets and teachers of the church at Antioch were Barnabas and Symeon (also called "The Black Man"), Lucius (from Cyrene), Manaen (the foster-brother of King Herod), and Paul. 2 One day as these men were worshiping and fasting the Holy Spirit said, "Dedicate Barnabas and Paul for a special job I have for them." 3 So

after more fasting and prayer, the men laid their hands on them—and sent them on their way." (Acts 13:1-3 TLB)

God used these relationships to confirm the call on Paul and Barnabas and to commend them into fresh grace for a new season of ministry and effectiveness which showed in the productive ministries they had among the Gentiles.

There are other instances in the Scripture when God used relationships to usher people into new seasons of life. Elijah did that for Elisha. Paul to Timothy. Pricilla and Aquila for Apollos, Peter for Cornelius, and vice versa. Meditate on the following passages for a greater understanding of this law of relationships.

Elijah and Elisha

"So Elijah went and found Elisha who was plowing a field with eleven other teams ahead of him; he was at the end of the line with the last team. Elijah went over to him and threw his coat across his shoulders and walked away again. 20 Elisha left the oxen standing there and ran after Elijah and said to him, "First let me go and say good-bye to my father and mother, and then I'll go with you!"Elijah replied, "Go on back! Why all the excitement?" 21 Elisha then returned to his oxen, killed them, and used wood from the plow to build a fire to roast their flesh. He passed around the meat to the other plowmen, and they all had a great feast. Then he went with Elijah, as his assistant." (1 Kings 19:19-21TLB)

Naomi and Ruth

"But Ruth replied, "Don't make me leave you, for I want to go wherever you go and to live wherever you live; your people shall be my people, and your God shall be my God; 17 I want to die where you die and be buried there. May the Lord do terrible things to me if I allow anything but death to separate us." 18 And when Naomi saw that Ruth had made up her mind and could not be persuaded otherwise, she stopped urging her. 19 So they both came to Bethlehem, and the entire village was stirred by their arrival." (Ruth 1:16-18 TLB)

Peter and Cornelius

"In Caesarea there lived a Roman army officer, Cornelius, a captain of an Italian regiment. 2 He was a godly man, deeply reverent, as was his entire household. He gave generously to charity and was a man of prayer. 3 While wide awake one afternoon he had a vision—it was about three o'clock—and in this vision he saw an angel of God coming toward him. "Cornelius!" the angel said 4 Cornelius stared at him in terror. "What do you want, sir?" asked the angel. And the angel replied, "Your prayers and charities have not gone unnoticed by God! 5-6 Now send some men to Joppa to find a man named Simon Peter, who is staying with Simon, the tanner, down by the shore, and ask him to come and visit you." 7 As soon as the angel was gone, Cornelius called two of his household servants and a godly soldier, one of his personal bodyguard, 8 and told them what had happened and sent them off to Joppa."

Later in the chapter, we see Peter caught up in a trance and God showing him foods that were considered non-kosher and instructing him to eat them. Peter refused, not knowing the food represented a new season in his ministry which would involve the opening up of a new territory for the church of taking the gospel to the Gentiles. A staple of Old Testament prophecy, this momentous, ground-breaking event in the history of the church was about to happen and it was ushered in by new relationships orchestrated by God.

"Peter was very perplexed. What could the vision mean? What was he supposed to do? Just then the men sent by Cornelius had found the house and were standing outside at the gate, 18 inquiring whether this was the place where Simon Peter lived! 19 Meanwhile, as Peter was puzzling over the vision, the Holy Spirit said to him, "Three men have come to see you. 20 Go down and meet them and go with them. All is well, I have sent them." 21 So Peter went down. "I'm the man you're looking for," he said. "Now what is it you want?" 22 Then they told him about Cornelius the Roman officer, a good and godly man, well thought of by the Jews, and how an angel had instructed him to send for Peter to come and tell him what God wanted him to do. 23 So Peter invited them in and lodged them overnight. The next day he went with them, accompanied by some other believers from Joppa." (Act 10:18-23 TLB)

Peter preached the gospel to them and they received the Holy Spirit, launching a new season in the history of the church. The questions to ask are: What if Cornelius had not listened to the angels? What if Peter had not received or followed the men sent from Cornelius? The story would have been different.

Satan likes to mimic God too, so you must be careful. Use this law to evaluate your relationships carefully. Watch the way you behave after you enter a new relationship. What season are you in? How did your thinking, speech, or actions change? What is happening around you as a result of this new relationship? Are you drawn closer to God or farther away from him? Are you making progress in your assignments for life or starting to slack and fall behind? The answers to these questions will help you pinpoint whether you are in a God-ordained relationship or you are bonding with a plant from the enemy.

Remember, relationships are territory openers and seasons changers. God uses them to bring rewards to you by giving you favor. Your prayers for new seasons and territories will be answered by new relationships. Your harvests of seed sown will come as "men give to your bosom, good measure, pressed down, shaken together and running over" (Luke 6:38 KJV). So be watchful for his orchestrations. The coming of your spring may be the new church you just joined or the new mentor you just met or the new friend you just made.

Part
2

The previous laws discussed focused on the importance and benefits of relationships. These new set of laws deal with the initiation of relationships.

CHAPTER

6

THE
LAW
OF
ORCHESTRATION

*God will arranges divine relationships for you
if you trust him to do so.*

"God causes the lonely to dwell in families..."
(Psalm 68:6 ISV)

Anyone who uses a computer or a word processor, or who visits websites like google or yahoo has experienced the use of the search engine. You can type a word into a search box in a word processor, click find, and it will bring out a result showing all the instance of that word within the document. Search engines like google, using more complex algorithms, do the same thing on a larger scale, scanning the world-wide web of millions of interconnected documents, and delivering results that match the imputed search phrase. The ability of these search engines to do these is because of the actions of automated robot programs called "crawlers" or "spiders" that scan the web and locate matches to the search words. These are indexed and presented to the user as the results.

Paul says the physical things in nature illustrate the invisible nature of God (Rom 1:20). While God cannot and should never be equated to an impersonal search engine, we can learn lessons about how God works from the way these programs work.

"For the eyes of the Lord search back and forth across the whole earth, looking for people whose hearts are perfect toward him, so that he can show his great power in helping them..." (2 Chronicles 16:9)

God's eyes scan the whole earth and he sees everyone. This means He can see, find, match, move, and connect people together in fitting with his plans. He can summon people from anywhere to accomplish his purpose. We have ample evidence of this in scriptures. For instance.

"From the east I summon a bird of prey; from a far-off land, a man to fulfill my purpose. What I have said, that I will bring about; what I have planned, that I will do." (Isaiah 46:11 NIV)

God did this to link Phillip and the Ethiopian Eunuch together.

"But as for Philip, an angel of the Lord said to him, "Go over to the road that runs from Jerusalem through the Gaza Desert, arriving around noon." So he did, and who should be coming down the road but the Treasurer of Ethiopia, a eunuch of great authority under Candace the queen. He had gone to Jerusalem to worship and was now returning in his chariot, reading aloud from the book of the prophet Isaiah. The Holy

Spirit said to Philip, "Go over and walk along beside the chariot." (Acts 8:26-29)

Irenaeus of Lyons, one of the early church fathers, wrote regarding the Ethiopian eunuch, that he eventually went into the continent Africa, in the regions of Ethiopia and preached Christ there. The gospel was introduced to a continent through a divinely orchestrated encounter. God is a specialist in bringing people together to fulfill his purpose.

Some people doubt this, especially some who are unmarried and have been seeking a mate for some time. As a result, they exert a lot of effort trying to find a marriage partner on their own, without depending on God. They need to understand that God is a matchmaker — the perfect matchmaker. He knows exactly how to bring people together. He has the ability to do so.

I was once meditating on the passage in Genesis where God created Eve and brought her to Adam when I saw the verbs used in the passage all showed the direct actions of God. God caused, took, closed, made, and brought. He acted directly to ensure the first marriage. He was the matchmaker.

"And the Lord God said, "It isn't good for man to be alone; I will make a companion for him, a helper suited to his needs…Then the Lord God caused the man to fall into a deep sleep, and took one of his ribs and closed up the place from which he had removed it, and made the rib into a woman, and brought her to the man." (Genesis 2:18, 21-22).

God orchestrates other relationship types too. He brings friends together. He arranges ministry helpers, career connections, business alliances, and more.

The revelation I received from meditating on this passage created a conviction in me that God, in His great love for me, and with His vantage point of seeing everyone on the face of the earth, is directly acting on my behalf to ensure I meet the right people needed to fulfill His plans for my life in every season. I am always on the lookout for His divine relationship orchestrations. I do not take meeting new people lightly. Whenever I meet a stranger, I usually ask myself whether this was one of those divine encounters.

However, just as God only made a presentation of Eve to Adam but never forced Adam to choose her, He does not force us into relationships. Instead, He makes presentations to us, creating the circumstances that allow us to meet people. Sometimes, He gives us instructions to link-up with someone just as He did with Phillip and the Eunuch. Sometimes He just creates a curiosity or a special desire in our hearts to link-up with someone else. It behooves us to yield to such promptings and arrangements to take advantage of God's relationship orchestrations.

Praying for Divine Relationships

Whatever God has revealed as His will, you have the right and responsibility to pray for. He wants His will to be done on earth as it is in heaven (Matthew 6:10). On this premise, you should pray regularly for divine relationships. Ask the Lord to continually bring the right people into your life for His will to be done in your life and on earth. This was what Abraham's servant did when he went on a quest to find a wife for Abraham.

"O Jehovah, the God of my master," he prayed, "show kindness to my master Abraham and help me to accomplish the purpose of my journey.13 See, here I am, standing beside this spring, and the girls of the village are coming out to draw water. 14 This is my request: When I ask one of them for a drink and she says, 'Yes, certainly, and I will water your camels too!'—let her be the one you have appointed as Isaac's wife. That is how I will know. As he was still speaking to the Lord about this, a beautiful young girl[named Rebekah arrived with a water jug on her shoulder and filled it at the spring. (Her father was Bethuel the son of Nahor and his wife Milcah." (Genesis 24:12-16 TLB)

Shortly after this prayer and the fortuitous encounter with Rebekah, this servant met with her parents and told them of his intent. They responded:

"Then Laban and Bethuel replied, "The Lord has obviously brought you here, so what can we say? 51.Take her and go! Yes, let her be the wife of your master's son, as Jehovah has directed." (Genesis 24:50, 51 TLB).

God obviously brought him to them. God orchestrated this divine connection in response to the prayer of Abraham's servant. His prayer in faith was an expression of trust in the God who can see all and can link people together miraculously.

If you want to experience the same in your life, cooperate with the law of orchestration. Make a habit of praying regularly for divine connections. Pray to God to help you meet your spouse, business partners, ministry partners, and destiny helpers. Soon you will start experiencing encounters with people that matter to your mission in life. Your life will be further enriched by this.

CHAPTER

7

THE
LAW
OF
INTENTIONALITY

Acquaintances may be accidental but relationships are made and built deliberately. Intentionality may require your repositioning.

"The man that has friends must show himself to be a friend, and there is a friend that sticks closer than a brother..."
(Proverbs 18:24 JUB)

Mary Kay Ash is quoted to have said there are three types of people in the world:

"Those who make things happen,
Those who watch things happen,
And those who wonder what happened."

We all fall into one of these groups of people, but in order for us to live the kind of life God desires for us we have to become intentional about creating it. To be intentional is to do things deliberately and on purpose. It is living by decision and not by default. When it comes to developing relationships, proactivity is a great virtue. Building relationships doesn't happen by accident. Relationships mature and are enhanced through intentional efforts. Someone has to make things happen.

Showing yourself to be a friend from Proverbs 18 is being intentional. It is taking the initiative to start the process of developing relationships. You take it upon yourself to do what is necessary to enrich your life with empowering relationships by seeking out new relationships and watering existing ones. Let's look at some ways you can practice intentionality in initiating relationships.

Intentional Positioning

"He who finds a wife finds what is good and receives favor from the LORD." (Proverbs 18:22)

Intentionality in relationships may involve a search. Although finding something may come unexpectedly or accidentally, it may require an active search process. In some of Jesus' parables, he spoke of active searches for a lost coin, sheep, and son to illustrate God's intentionality in pursuing a relationship with us. If God is that intentional, we should follow his example.

This involves positioning or repositioning ourselves deliberately to create greater possibilities of striking new empowering connections. It may sometimes require you to deliberately locate a company such as a network with a pool of the type of relationship you desire and then taking steps to join the network.

Knowing this principle has been of great benefit to Debo and I. We have several relationships that have been of tremendous blessings to us that came about because we intentionally reached out to or accepted invitations to join new networks or reactivate old ones.

We have joined ministers' associations and professional networks that have yielded profitable relationships. We have made wonderful friends in our children's schools PTA gatherings, our neighborhood associations, and more. Even though we are both not too fond of parties, we have intentionally gone to some that were made up of the kinds of people we desired to have relationships with. Intentionality in this manner has helped us break racial, cultural, and geographical barriers in relationships.

Intentional Communication

Another way we have practiced intentionality in beginning relationships is to reach out to people we desired relationships with through emails or phone calls. I recall many of the amazing mentors we have had in our life now came as a result of this. In those instances, God planted desires in our heart to cultivate relationships with these individuals. We knew of them but they did not know us. So we find their official contacts and reach out to them explaining our intentions. We got favorable responses. With additional intentional steps these relationships have become established and deepened.

Intentional Seeding

"Many seek favors from a ruler; everyone is the friend of a person who gives gifts!" (Proverbs 19:6)

I remember how I met one of my closest friends. He came from out of town with a guest minister we had invited. After the meeting, I felt the impression within me that we were to become friends. The Spirit of God instructed me to give an amount of money to him as a token of potential friendship. This was a freewill gift of appreciation and I did not even inform him of the impression I had received that prompted the act.

This act opened the door to a very close friendship and accountability relationship that has lasted over eleven years at the time of this writing and has produced great fruits in both our lives, families, and ministries.

Jesus and Intentional Relationships

Whether it is with the Samaritan woman at the well, attending a party at Levi's house in order to be with the publicans and sinners he wanted to minister to, or giving Peter a boatload of fishes and calling him to follow, Jesus practiced intentionality in relationships. He practiced intentional positioning, communicating, and seeding. These relationships started by his intentionality yielded great fruits for the kingdom. Read the following passages and observe how intentional he was.

"He left Judea and departed again to Galilee. 4 But He needed to go through Samaria.5 So He came to a city of Samaria which is called Sychar, near the plot of ground that Jacob gave to his son Joseph. 6 Now Jacob's well was there. Jesus therefore, being wearied from His journey, sat thus by the well. It was about the sixth hour.7 A woman of Samaria came to draw water. Jesus said to her, "Give Me a drink." 8 For His disciples had gone away into the city to buy food." (John 4:3-7)

"After these things He went out and saw a tax collector named Levi, sitting at the tax office. And He said to him, "Follow Me." 28 So he left all, rose up, and followed Him. 29 Then Levi gave Him a great feast in his own house. And there were a great number of tax collectors and others who sat down with them. 30 And their scribes and the Pharisees[b] complained against His disciples, saying, "Why do You eat and drink with tax collectors and sinners?" 31 Jesus answered and said to them, "Those who are well have no need of a physician, but those who are sick. 32 I have not come to call the righteous, but sinners, to repentance." (Luke 5:27-31)

"So it was, as the multitude pressed about Him to hear the word of God, that He stood by the Lake of Gennesaret, 2 and saw two boats standing by the lake; but the fishermen had gone from them and were washing their nets. 3 Then He got into one of the boats, which was Simon's, and asked him to put out a little from the land. And He sat down and taught the multitudes from the boat. 4 When He had stopped speaking, He said to Simon, "Launch out into the deep and let down your nets for a catch." 5 But Simon answered and said to Him, "Master, we have toiled all night and caught nothing; nevertheless at Your word I will let down the net." 6 And when they had done this, they caught a great number of fish, and their net was breaking. 7 So they signaled to their partners in the other boat to come and help them. And they came and filled both the boats, so that they began to sink." (Luke 5:1-7)

I encourage you to walk in His footsteps. Identify potential profitable relationships. Reach out. Join a network that gives you the opportunity of meeting such people and, when you meet with them, communicate intentionally. Seed if directed. Your steps of faith will be rewarded.

CHAPTER

8

THE
LAW
OF
CONVERSION

*God-sent people often come as strangers or enemies.
Learn the process of conversion.*

"Do not forget to show hospitality to strangers, for
by so doing some people have shown hospitality
to angels without knowing it." (Hebrews 13:2)

Several years ago, I hosted a book reading at my house
for one of my books. A young man I had never met
before was the first to arrive. He informed me that
someone in my group had invited him for the event. We began
to chat and soon he joined us in setting up the place for the book
event. When the evening ended, we chatted a little bit more,
exchanged contact information, and promised to keep in touch.

Several days after this, I felt the prompting to email him to check on him. He responded and shortly afterwards, I was over at his apartment to see him. To cut the story short, this stranger I met on that day at my place eventually became a founding member of The CityLight Church in Chicago and has been my associate pastor for several years. Our families are now closest of friends and our partnership in ministry and life continues to grow. His is one of the many stories of strangers we have met that have been converted into covenant relationships. It is a regular occurrence in our lives.

There are also instances of people we have become close friends with whom, before we met, you would classify as antagonists or "enemies" either because of wrong impressions or theological and other differences. An example is one our close and profitable friendships who at first had the wrong impression that we would judge him because he had gone through a divorce as a minister of the gospel, but was surprised when I reached out to him, invited him over, and affirmed him.

The point of these examples is that close relationships do not start by being close. They come disguised. When you meet people God has sent into your life, they will be strangers. Some of them will even come with negative, preconceived notions about who you are from what they've heard from others about you. In fact, there will be instances when these strangers come with the wrong motives. It is your responsibility to sift through to see which of these encounters needs conversion into closer relationships.

There are meetings of people that came with lit neon signs indicating a profitable relationship was God-planned but which ended up not going anywhere because the initial sparks were not nurtured by the parties involved.

When I look at the empowering relationships God has blessed Debo and I with around the world, I can trace each one of them to a beginning point where we and/or the other party had to deliberately, through a series of actions, take the relationship to greater depths.

The Practice of Conversion in Relationships

The practice of hospitality is one key approach to converting strangers into friends. The text in Hebrews 13 refers to how Abraham showed great hospitality to some strangers who came to his tent. These strangers turned out to be angels sent by God. Abraham treated them well and later they became his ally in rescuing his nephew from the destruction of Sodom and Gomorra. Abraham converted strangers into friends by beginning with hospitality. When you make hospitality a habit, you will be ready for the next steps in the conversion process.

Here are a few more conversion steps you could take intentionally to orchestrate a deeper relationship with people after the first meeting. These often take place automatically, but the key is to start using them intentionally. I call them the 11 Commandments of Intentional Relationship Conversion. I use the acrostic CONNECTIONS.

Before you go ahead, though, a caveat is that there are no guarantees that any series of steps or formula will make everyone you meet want to be your friends, or that all relationships will go the distance. Also, relationships develop over varying lengths of time. Some deepen quickly while others take a while. However, following these guidelines increases the possibility of maturing new friendships.

C- Choose whether you want a relationship or not

When you meet someone, the continuation, deepening, or termination of the relationship begins with a choice. You have to make the determination that pursuing an ongoing relationship is a profitable thing with a view to your purpose in life. If the choice is to develop a relationship, clearly define your objective for the relationship. The type of relationship you desire will determine your subsequent approach. For instance, developing a relationship with a mentor will look different from that of a peer.

O- Orchestrate an initial rendezvous with them

If you have yet to meet them, initiate contact with them and ask for a meet up. If you have met them, ask for more meet ups. Meetings can merge people, passions, purposes, and plans. Spending time with people is the backbone of growing relationships. It is even better when the meetings are outside your regular routine places, such as work or school.

N- Never forget to enthusiastically ask for an exchange of numbers, emails, and other contact details in other to keep up with them.

While some may, a lot of people will not give you their personal contact details unless they are comfortable with you. Sharing of personal details is a step further in the development of the relationship. Ask if you could, and how and when it is best to contact them. Some people are phone people. Others are email or social media folks. People even have unique social media preferences.

N- Now breathe more life into the relationship through frequent contact.

Repeated hanging out, chatting, phone calls, emails, and continued communication using the preferred medium of the other party deepens relationships. Exercise discretion on the frequency, times, length, intent, and content of conversations. You can approach this by noting the following.

E- Express genuine interest in the other person's needs, wants, and dreams.

Don't center your conversations on yourself and your desires. People are mostly interested in themselves. Without pushing, give ample time in conversations for people to share about their passions and dreams. When you know what people desire, you know how to be their genuine friend by helping them accomplish their dreams. Show them you like being in their presence and that you are interested in what they have to say.

C- Converse on mutual topics of interest.

Another way to deepen the relationship is to discuss topics of mutual interest. Friendships develop there is a realization of commonalities. Career, sports, politics, science, art, and other topics of mutual interest have a way of giving people a kindred feeling which further strengthens connections.

T- Talk, tell, and talk more. Talk about yourself too.

While ensuring you don't make yourself the dominant topic of your conversations, sharing about yourself can further advance the relationship. People often connect deeper when they experience the other person demonstrate appropriate vulnerabilities. Also, we often see our own stories in that of another and shared experiences create buddies. Open up to them. As the relationship develops, go beyond the surface and talk more about more personal topics.

I- Invest in the relationship.

"A friend in need is a friend indeed" goes the adage. As you find out in conversations about the other party's needs and desires, make your resources available to them. Be there for them in challenging times. Help them as you can in furthering their dreams. This is one of the characteristics of covenant friendships. Be a good receiver too.

O- Organize periodic times of joint activities.

Invite them to come along with you to church, or on an

outing to watch a game, go on a vacation, have dinner, watch a movie, have a game night, and more. Shared enjoyable activities create bonds that no other means can duplicate. Doing life together straightens bonds.

N- Never be the initiator of the end of the connection, even if they are difficult.

Keep it going unless they tell you to stop or it becomes dangerous or affects you negatively.

S- Surround the entire process with prayers.

Jesus practiced these things in his relationship with his disciples:

1. He chose those he wanted to be with him. "And when day came, he called his disciples and chose from them twelve, whom he named apostles." (Luke 6:13),

2. He defined and expressed the purpose of the relationship, "Come, follow me," Jesus said, "and I will send you out to fish for people." (Matthew 4:19),

3. He met with them frequently. "… He said to them, "Come with me by yourselves to a quiet place and get some rest." (Mark 6:32)

4. He had conversations with them about them, himself, and other topics of mutual interest. "I no longer call you servants, because a servant does not know his master's business. Instead, I have called you friends, for everything that I learned from my Father I have made known to you." (John 15:15)

5. He invested in them. "And when he had finished speaking, he said to Simon, "Put out into the deep and let down your nets for

a catch… And when they had done this, they enclosed a large number of fish, and their nets were breaking" (Luke 5:4,6)

6. He did things with them. "After six days Jesus took Peter, James and John with him and led them up a high mountain, where they were all alone…" (Mark 9:2)

As you imitate Jesus in initiating and deepening relationships, may you see more empowering relationships multiply around you.

CHAPTER

9

THE
LAW
OF
BLANKETING

*Treat everyone honorably because you don't know
which one is an angel & all deserve honor*

"Show proper respect to everyone, love the family of
believers, fear God, honor the emperor." (1 Peter 2:17)

It has been amusing but also instructional to read of
several instances that a celebrity disguises themselves as
a homeless person on the streets and were amazed at the
responses they got from passersby.

For example, I read of one that took place at a Metro Station
in Washington D.C. in the winter of 2007. A man with a violin
played several Bach pieces for about 45 minutes. During the
period, out of the more than 1000 people that passed by and
heard him play, only seven stopped briefly to listen.

Twenty more gave money but never stopped. The violinist earned a total of $32.17. When he finished, there was no applause or recognition. None of the passersby knew that the violinist was Joshua Bell, one of the most accomplished musicians in the world, and that the violin he was using was worth $3.5 million dollars. A few days before this, Joshua Bell had played in a sold-out theater where people had paid an average of $100 to hear the same music he was playing at the Metro Station.

Reading the story, I wondered what would have happened to someone who had stopped briefly to talk to, or tried to befriend the unknown violinist. It was definitely a missed opportunity for many. How many Joshua Bells do we miss as we hurry through life, paying little attention and giving little or no honor to people who don't strike us as important?

A Blanket of Honor

To "blanket" means to cover all — to be total and inclusive in approach. The law of blanketing addresses the treating of everyone with honor irrespective of who they are.

Peter exhorts us to blanket everyone with respect. Jesus admonishes that we should not only greet those we perceive can offer us some reciprocal advantage, but to honor all, following our Heavenly Father's example of blanketing everyone, both good and evil, with his sun and rain.

"You have heard that it was said, 'You shall love your neighbor and hate your enemy.' 44 But I say to you, Love your enemies and pray for those who persecute you, 45 so that you may be sons of your Father who is in heaven. For he makes his sun rise on the evil and on the good, and sends rain on the just and on the unjust. 46 For if you love those who love you, what reward do you have? Do not even the tax collectors do the same? 47 And if you greet only your brothers, what more are you doing than others? Do not even the Gentiles do the same? 48 You therefore must be perfect, as your heavenly Father is perfect. (Matthew 5:43-48)

We rise to the level of God's attitude toward people when we make it a practice to give honor to everyone we meet whether they deserve it or not. Jesus also implies there is a reward for treating people, especially those we feel are underserving, with respect.

Meeting People's Greatest Craving

Dale Carnegie in his phenomenal book, *How to Win Friends and Influence People*, identified the need to feel important as one of the deepest cravings of people. Everyone wants to be honored and appreciated and they will go to great extents to meet this need. This deep craving is responsible for much of the accomplishments, feats of prowess, and creativity that abound in the world now. It is the reason why people want to associate with certain people and groups, take on titles of honor, and even do acts of charity. We all crave significance.

The way this craving is met is by giving sincere appreciation and recognition. This doesn't refer to flattery but to the genuine appreciation and honor of everyone you meet.

Honor's Reward

Honor's reward is honor for the person who practices it. Whenever we honor what God honors, we are honoring him, and there is a reward for honoring him. He said,

> "...those who honor me I will honor, and those who despise me shall be lightly esteemed." (1 Samuel 2:30)

To be successful in relationships, you need honor from God. Treating everyone honorably and genuinely is sowing seeds of honor. It will produce fruits. Let everyone you meet feel significant because of how you treated them. Appreciate people genuinely. Give them a feeling of importance. Carnegie wrote that the person who masters this skill will "hold people in the palm of his or her hand and 'even the undertaker will be sorry when he dies.'"

How to Practice the Law of Blanketing

1. Treat everyone equally with honor regardless of how they appear or the situation you meet them in. Don't look down on anyone.

2. Practice walking slowly through the crowd. Pause to greet people and look at them in the eye when you do.

3. Develop the habit of sincerely appreciating and complimenting people. Find something to appreciate even if their behavior or situation makes it difficult.

4. Give the gift of significance by asking for and remembering their names.

4. Honor people with your full attention when they speak.

5. Demonstrate grace. Avoid being critical of people

Practice the Law of Blanketing continually. The rewards will manifest as great and empowering relationships all around you. And who knows? One could be a fortuitous encounter with an angel in disguise.

CHAPTER
10

THE
LAW
OF
THE CIRCLES

There are levels of relationships and not everyone is at the same level with you. The choice of who occupies your innermost circles is yours to make. Relationships should never be forced on you.

"And he went up on the mountain and called to him those whom he desired, and they came to him. And he appointed twelve (whom he also named apostles) so that they might be with him and he might send them out to preach."
(Mark 3:13-14 ESV)

O ne day, a farmer took his shot gun to shoot at some crows that were causing a disturbance around the farm. Unknown to him, his parrot had joined the crows earlier.

After firing some shots, he went over to check the fallen birds and, to his surprise, he found his parrot among them with one of its wings broken. Later, when the farmer's children asked what caused the injury to the parrot, the farmer simply replied, "Bad company."

The source of this story is unknown, but it again underscores the importance of treating the choice of your company seriously. We already discussed the implications of the company we keep in the chapter on the Law of Impartation. The Law of the Circles places the responsibility of the type of company you keep on you and unveils the privilege to select the right people to be part of your inner circles.

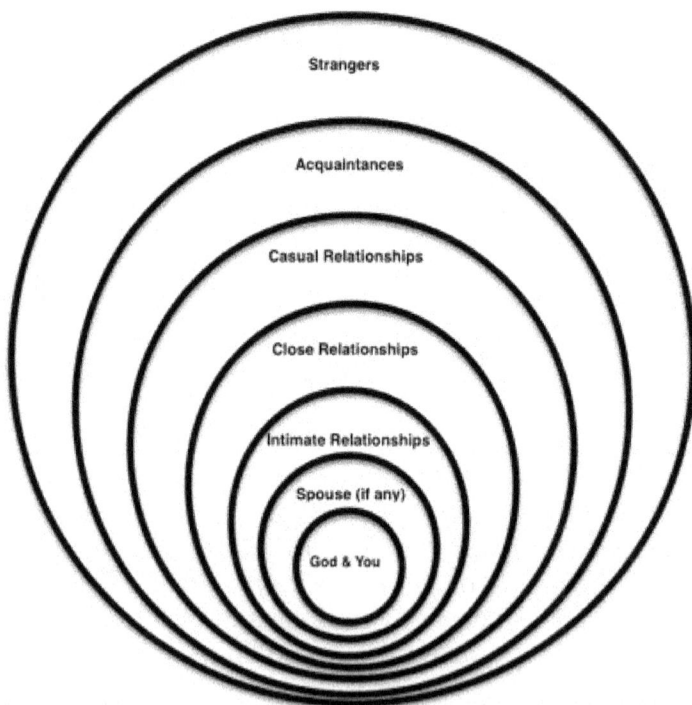

Since your relationships will have considerable impact on your destiny, the choice of who you allow or not is yours to make. You will be presented with many options, but it is your responsibility to wisely choose the level you will allow people to go with you in relationships.

Levels of Relationships

The levels of relationship you allow people to have with you can be represented by a series of concentric circles. Each level comes with certain responsibilities and privileges. It is important to define which level people are at with you in order to manage your expectations of them and theirs of you.

Strangers

These are people you meet but have no relationship with. An example is someone you just met at the airport lounge or that was just introduced to you by a friend. The expectations at this level are minimal. The Bible commands hospitality (Hebrews 13:2), or assistance if they are in need, as in the case of the Good Samaritan story told by Jesus (Luke 10:25-37). Your discussions with strangers are on a superficial level, not advancing beyond trivial like sport, weather, politics, or any other current happenings. If you feel comfortable with someone at this level, you might choose to bump them to the next level if they desire the same.

Acquaintances

At this level, things are still superficial, though a little deeper than the stranger level. You are getting to know the person. You may share some of your feelings, but keep them largely non-intimate, positive, and uncontroversial.

Casual Relationships

At this level, you have discovered things you have in common with the person. You are beginning to share deeper things such as your goals, plans, life-stories, or desires. You are more comfortable and free in the person's company, and can share some negative things. Be genuine. Treat the information shared with you with respect. Pray for this person.

Close Relationships

If a casual relationship grows, it moves to this level, though it usually takes time. Here, you have realized you share similar goals and values in life. You share deeper information about yourselves, though not everything. You pray together and comfortably play together. You are familiar with most of the details of one another's lives. Close relationships have gone beyond mental and emotional connections into the spiritual arena. Many of your relationships will remain at this level.

Intimate Relationships

This level takes a while to reach. People at this level have been friends for a considerable amount of time. The relationship has been tested as it went through various seasons of life, good, bad, and ugly. It has become a covenant relationship with extreme reliability on one another. It is this level that Proverbs 18:24 refers to: "a friend that sticks closer than a brother." You have experienced the worst of each other. You know to a very high degree most things about each other and have become the best of friends. This level comes with higher responsibilities. It calls for openness, accountability, honesty, loyalty, confidentiality, unwavering support, investments in one another, and more. You should be able to confront and correct one another.

Spousal Relationships

This is a special kind of exclusive intimate relationship which also has the highest reward and responsibilities of all relationship with humans. It is the closest bond one can have with another human in this life and it comes with the gift of sex, the greatest bonding experience that exists. Genesis describes the depth of intimacy this way: "And the man and his wife were both naked and were not ashamed" (Genesis 2:25). At this level of relationship, the entire beings of the two involved completely merge together into one. The two become one flesh (Genesis 2:24).

God and You

This innermost circle consists of you and God alone. It is the center and driving force of your life and relationships. No one, not even your spouse should encroach on this space. It comes with the greatest benefit and responsibilities of all relationships. A healthy relationship with God helps you succeed in other relationships. It is cultivated in the secret place of prayer, study, and meditation in God's word. The goal is to "Love the Lord your God with all your heart and with all your soul and with all your strength and with all your mind" (Luke 10:27). Prioritize this above all.

Jesus had his circles too. He had the multitudes, the seventy, the twelve, the three (Peter, James, and John), John who reclined on his bosom (John 13:23), and his relationship with the Holy Spirit. There were things the Holy Spirit shared with him that he could not tell anyone (John 16:12), and there were things he restricted to the three (Matthew 17:9), and some to the disciples (Matthew 13:11).

Be deliberate about your relationships. Let each one be purposeful and well defined. With God's direction, let your relationships with people move from the outer circles to the inner circles gradually. Don't jump circles or you will skip many important lessons and boundaries and it may become detrimental to the relationship. Prober bonding involves going from level to level as people qualify.

And in conclusion, never forget the Law of the Circles also implies that, with the exception of your relationship with God, and only in certain restricted scenarios of the spousal relationship, if a relationship becomes detrimental to your walk of purpose, you have the right to terminate it no matter what levels they have advanced to. Choose wisely!

Part

3

*The following laws deal with building
and harnessing relationships.*

CHAPTER

11

THE
LAW
OF
PRIORITIES

The quality of your horizontal relationships is influenced by your vertical relationship.

But seek first the kingdom of God and his righteousness, and all these things will be added to you." (Matthew 6:33 ESV)

You may be familiar with the illustration popularized by Stephen Covey, the author of the *7 Habits of Highly Effective People*. Imagine you have a jar full of big rocks, a jar of pebbles, a jar of sand, and a jar of water. You want to put everything into one jar. In what order will you put them.

If you said, "put the big rocks in first, shake the pebbles, and then the sand around the rocks, and then pour the water in on top" you are right. Any other order and something will not fit. The point is this: If you don't put the big rocks in first, you'll not be able to get them in at all, but if you put them in first, you will be able to get the others in.

When it comes to relationships, the biggest rock of all is your relationship with God. Investment in it has to be prioritized. When you do, its effects will trickle down into all your interactions with people and make them better. Those who are most successful on their knees are the best on their feet with people. Your friendship with God will make you a more fruitful person in your dealings with people.

A young man was working at a pawnshop. He never liked the work, but he did it faithfully until something better came along. He knew his real work was serving God in helping the poor, but in the meantime, he had to do what he did. However, he made the following resolutions and wrote them on a scrap of paper.

"I promise God that I will rise early every morning to have a few minutes—no less than five—in private prayer. I will endeavor to conduct myself as a humble, meek, and zealous follower of Jesus, and by serious witness and warning, I will try to lead others to think of the needs of their immortal souls. I hereby vow to read no less than four chapters in God's Word every day. I will cultivate a spirit of self-denial and will yield myself a prisoner of love to the Redeemer of the world."

That young man was William Booth, the founder of the Salvation Army. Over a century after he made that commitment to prioritize his fellowship with God, the result of his work among men continues to abound.

God Has What We Lack in Relationships

Your relationship with people is often affected negatively by certain factors such as a lack of wisdom in addressing relational situations, your personal emptiness and need that makes you put heavy demands on people, the wrong evaluation of people, the lack of proper response to their actions and more. Dwelling consistently in fellowship with God helps you in these relational issues. He promised to fill you with his presence, wisdom, and grace. God can teach you how to be a better spouse, parent, friend, mentor, or student. He fills you so much with himself and his love and compassion rub off on you and become your own driving impulses too. He has what we lack and he's waiting to impart them to us as we prioritize friendship with him.

God-Shaped Needs

One of the best teachings on relationships I have heard was when Andy Stanley taught on James 4:1-2 at the Hillsong Conference in Sydney, Australia. It opened my eyes to certain things I had not seen before and has been very empowering to my relationships.

> "What causes quarrels and what causes fights among you? Is it not this, that your passions are at war within you? 2 You desire and do not have, so you murder. You covet and cannot obtain, so you fight and quarrel. You do not have, because you do not ask." (James 4:1-2)

Conflicts ensue in relationships because the parties involved have unmet needs. When attempts are made by the parties to have these needs met by one another and they still go unmet, quarrels and fights ensue. The problem with this approach is there are some needs in relationships that no human can meet.

They are God-shaped needs. Expecting people to meet them will always end in disappointment and lead to conflicts as pressure is put on people. James follows this diagnosis with the cure — go before God and ask for what you need. Only God can fill these God-shaped needs. Only God can truly provide fulfillment, joy, self-worth, and inner peace. People can't provide these.

Vertical First

So, making your vertical relationship with God a priority helps you enjoy your horizontal relationships with people. The better the former is, the more its effect on the quality of the latter. When your emptiness has been filled by God, the overflow of your heart will enrich your relationships. You will no longer see people as your source of anything. You become a giver and a distributor of grace in your interactions with people. This does not imply you will no longer have relational problems. There will be plenty of them, but you will be better equipped to handle them as they come with the wisdom of God.

Moses was with God and his face shone before the people. It was said of the disciples that people perceived they had been with Jesus when they saw their boldness.

> "Now when they saw the boldness of Peter and John, and perceived that they were uneducated, common men, they were astonished. And they recognized that they had been with Jesus." (James 4:13)

Jesus rose early in the morning to be with God before being with people. He said He did or said nothing except what He saw the Father do or say. No wonder he maximized His relationships for the purpose He was sent to fulfill on earth.

Thumbs Up

I love the following illustration. I think it is one of the best ways to explain how to practice the Law of Priority in relationships.

In the picture, the thumb represents your relationship with God. It points up as a reminder that your primary focus in relationships should be vertical and upward toward God. This focus on God gives you your identity, strength, and wisdom for other relationships. You apply all that you learn from Him in the other relationships.

Your other relationships, represented by the four other fingers, wrap around this primary relationship. The forefinger is your relationship with your spouse, the middle finger with your children, the ring finger with other believers, and your small pinky finger your relationship with the world — those not in Christ yet.

The order of these fingers helps you properly prioritize your relationships and underscores the importance of balance in relationships. All the fingers are necessary to properly grasp things. In the same way, all these relationships are essential for your effective functioning in life. As you prioritize your relationship with God, your other relationships will be blessed.

I will leave you with the following poem:

I got up early one morning and rushed right into the day!
I had so much to accomplish that I didn't take time to pray.

Problems just tumbled about me, and heavier came each task.
"Why doesn't God help me?" I wondered, He answered, "You didn't ask!"

I tried to come into God's presence; I used all my keys at the lock.
God gently and lovingly chided, "Why, child, you didn't knock!"

I wanted to see joy and beauty, but the day toiled on, gray and bleak.
I wondered why God didn't show me. He answered me, "But you didn't seek."

I woke up early this morning, and paused before entering the day.
I had so much to accomplish, that I had to take time to pray.

—Author Unknown

CHAPTER

12

THE
LAW
OF
THE GOOSE

*Relationships thrive and yield long-term benefits when fed
and nurtured, but die when exploited for instant or selfish gratifications.*

"Use your worldly resources to benefit others and make
friends Then, when your possessions are gone, they will
welcome you to an eternal home." (Luke 16:9 NLT)

There are many version of the story of the goose that laid
the golden eggs but I like this version by Vernon Jones
best:

A man and his wife had the good fortune to possess a goose

which laid a golden egg every day. Lucky though they were, they soon began to think they were not getting rich fast enough, and, imagining the bird must be made of gold inside, they decided to kill it in order to secure the whole store of precious metal at once. But when they cut it open they found it was just like any other goose. Thus, they neither got rich all at once, as they had hoped, nor enjoyed any longer the daily addition to their wealth.

Great relationships are like geese that lay golden eggs. They are valuable social capital. They will bring lots of good into your life. You will accomplish many great things through the support and partnership of good friends. When these relationships are properly fed and nurtured, they continue to thrive and yield amazing benefits that sometime last a lifetime. They can even continue into succeeding generations, as illustrated by the covenant friendship of David and Jonathan in 1 Samuel 18, or that of Jesus and His disciples that transcended the earthly life of Jesus, and continued his work after He had gone to heaven. However, when relationships are exploited for selfish reasons or pressured for instant gravitation, they experience sudden death. First, let's examine the benefits.

The Golden Eggs of Relationships

Healthy relationships produce benefits that touch on all the fabrics of existence. They have spiritual, emotional, intellectual, physical, social, and financial benefits. In previous chapters, we already discussed some of these benefits in greater detail. I list them here.

1. Companionship
2. Impartation
3. Challenge and motivation
4. Accountability
5. Support for life's seasons
6. Better mental, emotional, and physical health

7. Wealth and Resources
8. Credibility and Endorsements
9. Liesure partners
10. Shared experiences
11. Wisdom and counsel
12. Platforms and sounding boards
13. Expanded networks
14. Correction and feedback to compensate for personal blindspots
15. Posterity and legacy

Great friends are used by God to assist you in the fulfillment of your purpose on earth. They will open doors, create opportunities, provide platforms, cheer you on, introduce you to new people, inspire you, challenge you, and fight alongside you. These are just a few of the benefits relationships that are properly nurtured can provide for you. The more intentional and proficient you become in initiating, nurturing, and harnessing relationships, the more these benefits manifest in your life.

Feeding the Goose

Jesus said to make friends with worldly resources. This statement by Jesus in Luke 16 was preceded by the story of the unfaithful steward who was about to be fired by his boss, but who used the opportunity of his current position as a steward to find out what his boss's clients owed him, and then proceeded to do favors for them by reducing the amount they owed. Jesus called this steward shrewd for taking this approach but lamented how children of the kingdom do not use the resources they have to faithfully accomplish their goals.

The key to nurturing relationships is to invest in them unselfishly. Keep looking for ways to be genuinely valuable to your friends. This is how you feed a relationship.

I take this commandment of Jesus to make friends with worldly resources very literally. I constantly inventory my resources to identify things I can use to bless my friends. It could be as simple as a word of encouragement in a text message, a thoughtful personal message on their birthdays, a share of their social media post, endorsement of their causes in my sphere of influence, linking them with opportunities and other relationships, supporting their dreams, offering a listening ear, or traveling over long distance to be with them during important moments of life. In practicing this over the years, I have seen our relationships deepened and grow and I have enjoyed numerous investments of people in my own life in return.

Slaughtering the Goose

I have observed how relationships wither when one or more of the individuals involved tries to selfishly exploit the relationship at the expense of others. Selfishness and greed kill the goose. A one-sided relationship in which only one person enjoys the benefit at the expense of others is parasitic. No one wants to continue living with a parasite. They want to be rid of it.

I remember a "friend" I had once that so pressured our relationships with demands that it killed it. Almost every time we talked, he was either requesting financial assistance or complaining about how I had not called or visited in a long time but had neglected him for other friends. Our conversations were dominated by his request for one thing or the other. For some time, I tried all I could to meet these demands because I wanted the relationship to work, but eventually, I could not handle the pressure anymore. I had to withdraw from the relationship. The goose was stressed out and it died!

Invest in your relationships. Use your worldly resources to make friends. Whatever you hope to get from relationships, put that in it and keep your fingers crossed. Be a dependable friend. Add value to people and you will become valuable. Don't put pressure on the relationship to meet your own needs. Focus on the needs of others. Feed the goose. It will yield golden eggs and you will enjoy it for a long time.

CHAPTER

13

THE
LAW
OF
RECIPROCITY

Give into relationships what you want from it. You will reap what you sow somewhere, sometime.

"Do to others as you would like them to do to you."
(Luke 6:31 NLT)

"Never criticize or condemn—or it will all come back on you. Go easy on others; then they will do the same for you. For if you give, you will get! Your gift will return to you in full and overflowing measure, pressed down, shaken together to make room for more, and running over. Whatever measure you use to give—large or small—will be used to measure what is given back to you." (Luke 6:37-38 TLB)

G rowing up in Africa, one of the first things I was introduced to in life was agriculture. From a very early age, my dad introduced me to the concept of planting seeds, nurturing them, seeing them grow, and yielding fruits. I still remember days when we hunted for humus soil in more fertile terrains, packed them in buckets, then carried them home to use in our little garden at the back of our house. I remember visits to my grandfather's cocoa farms, working in the sun with my dad, and learning from him about the amazing ability of nature that turns tiny seeds into giant trees. I planted beans, corns, and vegetables and saw them grow to yield edible and marketable fruits. I kept poultry and a few other small animals and saw them mature, lay eggs, and yield offsprings.

When I began studying and teaching the Bible in earnest, this background in agriculture helped me understand and appreciate a principle that permeates the entirety of Scripture — the principle of reciprocity—or seed-harvest as some call it. It is also called the law of compensation. The law simply states that all we do and say are seeds planted into the soil of nature, and which eventually come back to us in multiplied form. I knew this was true in farming, so it wasn't difficult to extrapolate the law to all of life, including to relationships.

Nature, A Giant Soil

In the beginning of it all, God revealed that all of nature is a giant soil that produces after its kind. The Law of Reciprocity is the Fundamental Law of Nature that governs everything.

"And God said, "Let the earth sprout vegetation, plants yielding seed, and fruit trees bearing fruit in which is their seed, each according to its kind, on the earth." And it was so. 12 The earth brought forth vegetation, plants yielding seed according to their own kinds, and trees bearing fruit in which is their seed, each according to its kind… And God said, "Let the earth bring forth living creatures according to their kinds—livestock and creeping things and beasts of the earth according to their kinds."

And it was so. 25 And God made the beasts of the earth according to their kinds and the livestock according to their kinds, and everything that creeps on the ground according to its kind. And God saw that it was good. 26. Then God said, "Let us make man in our image, after our likeness." (Genesis 1:11,12, 24-26)

The earth was commanded by God to bring forth vegetation and creatures according to their kinds. When God wanted to create man too, He commanded himself to bring forth after his image and likeness—His kind. Later, He commanded mankind to do the same. Listen carefully, nature is under God's command to produce whatever is sown into it after its kind. We know this concerning farming, and animal and human reproduction, but many are unaware that the law extends to words, thoughts, emotions, and actions. *EVERYTHING produces after its kind.* He also commanded mankind to be fruitful.

The best thing that can happen to an apple seed is not that it is eaten or thrown away, but that it is planted. If it is planted, then it has a chance to produce an apple tree which produces more apples. If it goes through that process of being planted and begins to yield more apples, it is said to be fruitful. Fruitfulness is the ability of a thing to reproduce itself.

God blessed and commanded them to be fruitful. In other words, God empowered them to reproduce themselves. God was saying that in them, He had invested His dream for the earth, which is to see it filled and subdued, but that dream was placed in them as seeds that must be planted before it became a reality. Adam and Eve were walking houses of God's dream. Billions of humans were in them in potential seed form. They were to get involved in the reproductive process of planting these seeds, replicating themselves over and over.

You are not exempted from this law. You too are a walking house of the seeds of God's dream for a part of the earth. You are a seed planted by God in the earth. Everything you are, that is in you or in your life now, is a seed. Your physical life, thoughts, word, talents, experience, love, strength, habits, possessions, relationships, knowledge, and every other thing in your life now is a seed. Everything you will ever be is already in your life now in potential form. God never needs to do anything new for humans, animals, or plants to reproduce themselves. All they have to do is engage in His established process. In the same way, you only need to get in His process of planting and replicating.

Sowing in Relationships

Jesus reiterated this law in the opening Scriptural passage of this chapter, applying it to relationships. Criticism will produce after its kind, forgiveness will generate forgiveness, love will attract more love, honor more dishonor, support and empathy will generate more in your direction. It works for both negative and positive inputs since the law does not discriminate. EVERYTHING produces after its kind, for EVERYONE, EVERY TIME!

Sow how do you apply The Law of Reciprocity in relationships?

Become Seed-Minded

It starts by becoming seed-minded in every area of life. Plant knowledge by sharing it. Plant your faith by sharing it. Plant your finances by investing them in loving God and others. Plant your dreams by diligently working on them. Plant good thoughts and words in your life. Plant good habits. Remember, everything is blessed to be fruitful. Don't be intimidated by how little things look in your life now. Think like a farmer. The process works indiscriminately. Even bad seeds are blessed to reproduce. Whatever a man sows, he will reap. Never forget. Your future is already in your life now, waiting to be planted. Plant it.

Invest in People

"Whatever you make happen for others, God will make happen for you" - Mike Murdock

"You will get all you want in life, if you help enough other people get what they want." - Zig Ziglar

These two quotes are apt ways of communicating the application of the Law of Reciprocity in relationships. Give into relationships what you want from them. Treat others as you would want to be treated. Serve and help people joyfully. While you are doing this, be careful not to focus your expectations on receiving from the people you are helping. That would be bribery or manipulation. Help because it would help. Give because it would make a difference. Serve because that's what you do.

So, get up and sow love. Give opportunity to others. Forgive them. Encourage them. Sow the feeling of significance into their lives by appreciating them profusely. Sow honor. Support their dreams and visions. Give finances to those in need and into their worthy causes. When you make sowing seeds like these your regular practice, you set the Law of Reciprocity into motion and it will cause a return to come to somewhere, some time later. You may not reap from where you sow but you will reap what you sow.

CHAPTER

14

THE
LAW
OF
THE CENTER

The world doesn't revolve around you. Earth's population with one exception consists of others. To have fulfilling relationships, the center must shift away from you to others.

"Let each of you look not only to his own interests, but also to the interests of others." (Philippians 2:4)

I like collecting nice quotations, poems, and pithy sayings. I came across this one recently. I thought it was a fitting beginning to this chapter.

On Getting Along With People

The SIX most important words:

"I admit I made a mistake."
The FIVE most important words:
"You did a good job."
The FOUR most important words:
"What do you think?"
The THREE most important words:
"After you please."
The TWO most important words:
"Thank you."
The ONE most important word:
"We"
The LEAST important word:
"I"

(Source Unknown.)

We all have the natural tendency to be self-centered. Need proof? When you see a group photo with you in it, whose picture do you look for first? Whose pictures appear the most on your Facebook or Instagram profiles? Did you know that the Oxford English Dictionary word of the year for 2013 was "selfie" and that twitter declared 2014 as the year of the selfie? Which word do you think is one of the most used in spoken and written conversations? If you said "I", you guessed right.

In his revealing book, *The Secret Life of Pronouns: What Our Words Say About Us*, social psychologist and language expert, James W. Pennebaker, from the computational analysis of an extensive amount of written and spoken texts, ranked "I" as the top most frequently used word in written and spoken text.

Self-interest is not necessarily a bad thing. We have a responsibility to look to our own interests. We need a healthy measure of self-focus to fulfill our natural duty of self-care and to take responsibility for our assignments in life. However, when it becomes untempered, rising to the level of an obsession with self at the expense of others, it becomes detrimental to us and to our relationships. If we become the gravitational center of everything in our world, where all roads lead to us and our self-interests, we become locked in our little, ever-shrinking worlds.

"The world of the generous gets larger and larger; the world of the stingy gets smaller and smaller." (Proverbs 11:24 MSG)

Considering earth's population, you are certainly outnumbered. It is a big world out there. The Law of the Center postulates that, in order to keep growing and have healthy relationships, the center of your world must shift from you. You have to become as interested in people as you are in yourself and your desires.

Self-Centeredness in Relationships

Self-centeredness manifests itself in various unhealthy ways in relationships. It is important to examine yourself to see if you display these traits. Also, because many self-centered people are completely unaware of their tendencies, it may require you to ask others who are in close relationships with you to give you a candid assessment of your behavior. Here are some ways self-centeredness manifests in a person.

1. This World of Mine

A self-focused person thinks the world is about them. To them, it is a place consisting of themselves, their interests, and people who have been created to serve their interests. They live inside this bubble and do everything to keep it from bursting. They are lost in it and oblivious to the needs of others.

2. This View of Mine

Self-absorbed people do not see the world from the perspectives of others. They believe they see the world in high definition and it is the only accurate view. Every other person is seeing wrongly. They are very opinionated.

3. This Turf of Mine

A self-focused person is very defensive. They fight tooth and nail to protect their image, flaws, and opinions. They hide who they are and keep people out. Sometimes they do this by safely guarding their vulnerabilities, never discussing them, while projecting their successes instead. They may not be able to keep lasting relationships because they keep pushing people out of their lives who threaten their turf.

4. This Toy is Mine

Have you seen little kids fight to hold on to toys, sometimes even when they're not theirs? That's exactly how self-centered people fight to hold on to things. Generosity is difficult for a self-absorbed person. They are very selfish. They only give if there is a possibility of getting more or use the gift to control others. To them, relationships are tools for getting more.

5. You are Mine

Self-absorbed people are very imposing and controlling. They use relationships to hold others down and keep them in line with their own wishes. They think they are superior to others and act that way.

6. Yours Should be Mine

Self-centered people do not respect boundaries. Since the world is all about them, everything in it should be theirs. They are not content with what they have, but they have a desire to claim what belongs to others. They are very envious. Whatever good is happening to other people saddens them because it is not about them. They are unable to celebrate another person's success sincerely. Whatever they can't get credit for, they criticize or avoid.

7. Mine is Mine

Self-focused people don't want people sharing in or benefiting from their possessions or accomplishment. The limelight is theirs alone. They take full responsibility for their success and complete ownership of the rewards. If it succeeds, they did it. If it fails, they find someone else to blame.

8. As Long as I Got Mine

Self-centered people lack empathy. The only pain they know is theirs. The only joy that matters is theirs. As long as they are ok, the world can go to hell in a hand basket.

9. Let's Talk About Mine

Self-interested people ensure they are the continual topic of conversations. They are always directing conversation to themselves and their interests. They can be arrogant. Talks with them are dominated by them bragging about themselves and their latest feats. They leave little or no room for other topics in their conversations.

10. The Spotlight is Mine

Finally, self-centered people are self-promoting, usually overexposed, and competitive. They cannot be second. Whoever is above them has to go down so they can claim the spotlight.

This list of characteristics of self-centered people is not all-inclusive, and people manifest these in varying degrees. There are mild expressions of them and, on the other side, extremely narcissistic people. The list is, however, enough for you to use in assessing yourself to see whether you are a self-centered person or you are involved in a relationship with one. Here's how to start shifting the center of your relationships from yourself to others.

Turning Outwards

"Love never gives up. Love cares more for others than for self. Love doesn't want what it doesn't have.Love doesn't strut, Doesn't have a swelled head, Doesn't force itself on others, Isn't always "me first," (1 Corinthians 13:4-5 MSG)

The antidote to selfishness is love. Love shifts the center of your world to others. It trades places with people, and places itself in people's shoes, then acts accordingly in ways that will benefit them. This type of love that Paul describes has been poured out into the hearts of every believer (Romans 5:5). It is the heart nature of every believer because we have been made into new creations after the image of God who is love. It is in you, so you only have to let it lose into your relationships. It will turn you outwards and beat self-centeredness every time.

Conditioning Yourself To Love

The way to unleash God's love in you is to start seeing yourself as naturally loving and then act out this conviction. I know of no better way to do this than prayerfully taking the passage on love in 1 Corinthians 13 and other love passages, personalizing it, and repeating it to yourself often until they are ingrained in your spirit. A great tool that can help you is my Bible app on the Apple Appstore and Google Play Store named ToYouBible which automatically personalizes passages of Scripture with your name. It also has a search functionality to locate passages by keywords.

Meditate on these love passages and practice them whether you feel like it or not. For instance, if you read that "love cares about others more than self" start saying that about yourself. Say, "I care about others more than myself," then deliberately put this into practice, doing something to show you care for someone else around you. Take time to listen to others, to ask questions, and to contribute to their well-being. You will start growing in love.

The Law of the Center says it is the people who show genuine interest in others and care about them that will have the most fulfilling relationships. Those who keep themselves as the center will live in ever-shrinking worlds from which springs all failures.

CHAPTER
15
THE
LAW
OF THE
LIFEBLOOD

*Communication is the life-blood of every relationship. It
must keep flowing. Without it, relationships wane and die.*

"My dear brothers and sisters, take note of this:
Everyone should be quick to listen, slow to
speak and slow to become angry." (James 1:19)

O
k. It's time for one more of the funnies. Here we
go:

Letter From College

Dear Dad,

$chool i$ really great. I am making lot$ of friend$ and

$tudying very hard. I $imply can't think of anything I need, $o if you would like, you can ju$t $end me a card, a$ I would love to hear from you.

Love,
Your $on

The Reply:

Dear Son,

I kNOw that astroNOmy, ecoNOmics, and oceaNOgraphy are eNOugh to keep even an hoNOr student busy. Do NOt forget that the pursuit of kNOwledge is a NOble task, and you can never study eNOugh.

Love,
Dad

Did that make you chuckle as it did me? Heads up, though, it has nothing to do with what I am sharing in this chapter, except that I like it, and it happens to be a funny illustration of how communication, the subject of this chapter, can be subtle. Let's get to the real serious stuff, though!

The Law of the Lifeblood has to do with the flow of communication in a relationship. Communication in relationships is the process of exchanging information between the involved parties. Just as the blood flow in a living organism carries life to all its parts and keeps them alive, a relationship is only as healthy as the communication flow, and if there is no flow, there is no relationship.

Types of Communication in Relationships

Verbal Communication
This involves the use of spoken words, language, and sounds.

Fluency in communicating verbally contributes to building better relationships.

Non-Verbal Communication

Non-verbal communication uses the other senses. Imagine all you can learn from someone's tone of voice, smile, frown, and body language (such as crossing their legs or arms, or looking down or away). How about their body odor or cologne smell? The majority of our communication occurs in the non-verbal arena. To strengthen relationships, you need to develop in this area.

Written Communication

The joke at the beginning of this chapter is an example of this—even this entire book. Emails, text messages, poetry, WhatsApp chats, Facebook statuses, Twitter posts, or a simple written note are all examples of written communication. Imagine what a simple note in a thank you card can do to a relationship. The unique thing about written communication is that you may not be able to take back what you have written and they can be stored and re-experienced at any time by the receiver. It is also difficult to put emotions and facial expressions in them. Hence the use of emoticons. All this says that written communication must be used carefully and wisely.

Visual Communication

It is said that a picture is worth a thousand words. Visual communication include things like photographs, symbols, logos, videos, snapchats, catalogs, and more. Visual communication can be very powerful in relationships. Imagine what posting a nice and happy picture of you and a friend on Instagram can do or what a nice profile picture on Facebook says.

Maintaining a Healthy Flow of Communication in Relationships

The discussed types of communication are to be engaged in strengthening your relationship. In order to use them effectively, consider the following advice on communicating well, mainly from the book of Proverbs.

The Style of Communication

"Whoever blesses his neighbor with a loud voice, rising early in the morning, will be counted as cursing." (Proverbs 27:14 ESV)

Everyone has their preferred style of communicating. Some people are more verbal while others are visual. Some prefer written communication, others a combination. It is important to know your own preferred style so you can inform your friends. You should also try to learn the preferred style of those in relationship with you. This helps you to maximize your communication. I prefer written communication to verbal, and I have found out that when I communicate in writing or read a written communication from a friend, I connect better. However, I am careful not to infer that this applies to all my friends. There are those who prefer a phone call.

The Timing of Communication

"Like golden apples in silver settings, so is a word spoken at the right time." (Proverbs 25:11 GW)

The timing of communication is very important. Imagine sharing the news about your promotion with a friend when he just lost his job or sending a joke to them when they just experienced a family loss. Now imagine you randomly text an inspiring quote to a friend while they were dealing with discouragement. Ask God to give you the tongue of the learned to know how to speak a word in season to the weary (Isaiah 50:4).

The Frequency of Communication

"Don't visit your neighbors too often, or you will wear out your welcome."
(Proverbs 25:17 NLT)

Too little or too much communication can affect relationships adversely. You will need to discern what regularity is appropriate for a particular relationship. It will vary depending on the stage and type of relationship. Communication with a busy mentor might be less frequent while chit-chats with a close or an intimate friend may be more.

The Volume of Communication

"A truly wise person uses few words a person with understanding is even-tempered." (Proverbs 17:27)

Another consideration in effective communication is the appropriate amount of information to be shared each time. Overloading people with information they are unable to process effectively is counterproductive. Giving too little may also work against the relationship. Imagine telling a friend to forgive you but refusing to tell them what you did wrong, or giving your spouse partial information about your financial state. Discretion is needed to discern the proper volume each time.

The Content of Communication

"Let your conversation be gracious and attractive so that you will have the right response for everyone." (Colossians 4:6 NLT)

A woman looked at her husband and asked him to describe her. He looked at her slowly without blinking and said: "ABCDEFGHIJK — Adorable, Beautiful, Cute, Delightful, Elegant, Fashionable, Gorgeous, Hot!" Then he stopped. The wife beaming, expecting more, asked what IJK stood for. He replied, "I'm Just Kidding." That's how the fight started.

It is a very useful skill in relationship to know what to say. Saying the right things at the right time, sending the perfect picture, or using the right gesture or body language for the moment is a relationship booster. The wrong content of communication can be fatal.

The Tone of Communication

"A soft answer turns away wrath, but a harsh word stirs up anger..." (Proverbs 15:1)

Not only is content important, the tone carries the content. It is said that "Please" has two tones, the sweet and the harsh. You could say "could you please pass me the bacon?" in either a pleasing or offensive tone. The occasion and goal of your communication should determine its tone. Sweet lips can work wonders. The wise of heart is called discerning, and sweetness of speech increases persuasiveness" (Proverbs 16:21).

The Depth of Communication

"A fool gives full vent to his spirit, but a wise man quietly holds it back." (Proverbs 29:11)

How deep you go in sharing your heart should be decided by the level of the relationship. Read the chapter on the The Law of the Circles again. Sharing intimate things too soon may work against the relationship. Your new friend may not know you enough to put the right context to what you are sharing and it may breed distrust. Also, you might not know the person enough to know what they will do with the information. Exercise self-control in this area. However, it is required you go deep and be transparent and vulnerable in intimate relationships. Hearts must touch hearts for their proper nourishing.

The Speed of Communication

"My dear brothers and sisters, take note of this: Everyone should be quick to listen, slow to speak and slow to become angry." (James 1:19)

Speaking is not necessarily communicating. Communication is what is heard. It is important to slow down to listen. The premier skill of a great communicator is listening.

The Power of Listening

"I like to listen. I have learned a great deal from listening carefully. Most people never listen." - Ernest Hemingway

"Nature gave us one tongue and two ears so we could hear twice as much as we speak." - Epictetus

I once read a story about Franklin Roosevelt. I am not sure if it is true or not, but it illustrates the importance of becoming a better listener. Roosevelt often endured greeting people who lined up to meet him at the White House and shake his hand. He observed that most people did not really pay attention to what he said as he greeted them, so on a particular day, he tried an experiment. As people passed by and shook his hand, he murmured to each of them, " I killed my grandmother this morning." The guests responded with words like, "Wonderful, that's great!" They all gave positive, encouraging responses. It was only at the end of the line, while greeting an ambassador that his words were actually heard. The ambassador leaned over and whispered, "I'm sure she had it coming."

Amusing as it may be, the story shows how most times we do not listen well enough. In order to keep the lifeblood of relationships flowing, you will need to be more aware of of others — their interests and aspirations. You cannot do this if you are the one continually dominating the conversation. You must become a better listener. It is as simple as becoming more curious about other people, their worlds and opinions, keeping an open, non-judgmental mind, asking questions and being observant. The better a listener you become, the better friend you are. The information you obtain through listening becomes your tool for investing in your relationships.

How to Be a Great Conversationalist

As I conclude this chapter, I wanted to pass this quick tip along to you. The secret of being a great conversationalist is not being eloquent or witty, though these have their place. The secret of great conversations is getting people to talk about what interests them. To pinpoint people's interest, you have to listen and ask questions. If you can get a pulse on someone's interests, you set them rolling when it is is brought up. They will do most of the talking and then they will thank you at the end for being a great conversationalist even though you hardly talked!

A Word About Fun and Laughter

"I'm struck by how laughter connects you with people. It's almost impossible to maintain any kind of distance, any sense of social hierarchy when you are just howling with laughter. Laughter is a force for democracy."
- John Cleese

An aspect of communication in relationship that has little to do with exchanging words is fun and laughter. When people play and laugh together, a deep form of connection takes place that bonds them faster than any other means. Many non-verbal exchanges take place when having fun together that are impossible to replicate in any other situation. People who play together, stay together.

Laughter subtly breaks the ice in relationships, builds bridges between hearts, and reduces tension. The more laughter there is in a relationship, the closer the people are. Create the time for fun and laughter in your relationships. It ensures the unhindered flow of the lifeblood.

I hope you develop more and more in practicing the Law of the Lifeblood. Your relationships will thank you for it.

CHAPTER

16

THE
LAW
OF
PROACTIVITY

Don't let the actions of others dictate your REACTIONS.
Let principles and values dictate your ACTIONS.

"To the contrary, "if your enemy is hungry, feed him; if he is
thirsty, give him something to drink…" (Romans 12:20 ESV)

I used the thermostat and the thermometer as an
illustration of influencing and being influenced in my
book, *Irresistible Influence: You Can Also Make a Difference.* I
think it is an appropriate way to begin this chapter.

The thermostat automatically regulates temperature by
turning on and off a device that provides either heat or cold to
a location. Whenever you adjust the temperature of your room,
you are using a thermostat. The thermometer, on the other hand,

measures temperature. A basic thermometer has a sensor within it, usually mercury or alcohol, that expands or contracts as the temperature varies, thus a temperature reading can be obtained on the scale. The thermostat acts on on the temperature in a room, while the thermometer reacts to it. When it comes to relationships, you should be like the thermostat, and not the thermometer.

Do You Carry Your Weather or Respond to the Weather?

In his book, *The Seven Habits of Highly Effective People*, Stephen Covey identified Habit #1 as "Be Proactive". He defined proactivity as being responsible for your own life, explaining that the word "responsibility" really is from "response-ability" which means to have the ability to choose your response. This comes from the fact that humans have the ability of self-awareness, something animals do not possess. We can know our thoughts, identify our moods, change them, decide on a chosen course of action, and so on.

The opposite of this is being reactive. Even though we have the ability to be proactive, we sometimes surrender this ability, allowing our environment or actions of others to rule us. According to Covey, reactive people are affected by the "social weather." When they are treated well, they feel good; when people treat them badly, they feel bad and respond by being defensive or protective. Their emotional lives are constructed around how others act toward them, thus unwittingly giving people power to control them.

Proactive people do the opposite. They carry their own weather with them. Even though they are still influenced by what goes on around them and how people act, they are driven by values, and they decide how to act informed by these values.

The Law of Proactivity

Ruling Your Spirit

"The man who has no refuge in himself, who lives, so to speak, in his front rooms, in the outer whirlwind of things and opinions, is not properly a personality at all. He floats with the current, who does not guide himself according to higher principles, who has no ideal, no convictions —such a man is a mere article of furniture—a thing moved, instead of a living and moving being— an echo, not a voice. The man who has no inner life is the slave of his surroundings, as the barometer is the obedient servant of the air at rest, and the weathercock the humble servant of the air in motion." - Henri-Frédéric Amiel

According to the The Law of Proactivity, the actions of others should not dictate your reactions. Instead, your principles and values should determine how you act. This is true power and control—control over yourself and what you chose to have power over you. True dominion is first rulership over your own spirit, actions, and responses. When you let others take control of that, you have surrendered your dominion.

"Whoever is slow to anger is better than the mighty, and he who rules his spirit than he who takes a city." (Proverbs 16:32)

Take Back Control

Taking back control starts with a decision to be in charge of your responses—to stop giving consent to people to hurt you. Yes, you cannot determine how others will act, but you can choose how you respond to them. You can choose to love when hated, to smile when persecuted, to lift up when you are put down. You can choose to feed an enemy when he's hungry, to walk away when someone picks a fight with you.

In the eyes of some, your chosen course of action might look like demonstrating weakness and allowing yourself to be taken advantage of, but the true demonstrators of power are those who are in control of their actions.

117

Being Proactive in Relationships

There are two types of instances where this law is highly applicable:

When You are Provoked

"You have heard the law that says the punishment must match the injury: 'An eye for an eye, and a tooth for a tooth.' But I say, do not resist an evil person! If someone slaps you on the right cheek, offer the other cheek also. If you are sued in court and your shirt is taken from you, give your coat, too. If a soldier demands that you carry his gear for a mile, carry it two miles." (Matthew 5:42 NLT)

When dealing with people who act negatively toward you, your choices are ether to respond in kind or otherwise. When you respond in kind to negative provocations, you give the other person control over you since you are the one responding to their initiative in the same terrain. They succeeded in dragging you into the mud with with them. If they are pigs, you are the loser even if you win the fight. Forgiveness falls in this category. When you choose to release someone who has hurt you, you are being proactive. While it could be tough to keep in these situations, The Law of Proactivity dictates that you choose your response based on your values, not theirs. Ghandi said, "They cannot take away our self respect if we do not give it to them." Win by using the provocation to demonstrate your values, not theirs. That's control!

When it is Deliberately Invoked

"One day David asked, "Is anyone in Saul's family still alive—anyone to whom I can show kindness for Jonathan's sake?" (2 Samuel 9:1)

The sweetest spot of the Law of Proactivity is when unprovoked, you choose to act favorable toward a person, especially someone who does not deserve it or who wasn't expecting it. You could choose to send a gift to someone, cut the grass for your neighbor, send a friend a word of encouragement, or ask to babysit for a friend. The looks on the faces of the recipients and their appreciation to God alone will make your day. These unprovoked actions of love not only will bless you, but will enrich your relationships.

It's time to be the thermostat in your relationships. I hope you are getting some crazy ideas on how you can have fun with this law right now!

CHAPTER 17

THE LAW OF THE LOG

Others aren't the initial problems to fix in your
relationships, you are. Positive change in relationships
come by focusing on changing the person in the mirror first.

"Why do you see the speck that is in your brother's eye, but do not notice the log that is in your own eye? Or how can you say to your brother, 'Let me take the speck out of your eye,' when there is the log in your own eye? You hypocrite, first take the log out of your own eye, and then you will see clearly to take the speck out of your brother's eye." (Matthew 7:2-5 ESV)

As I write this chapter, I'm humming under my breath the chorus of Micheal Jackson's famous song, "Man in the Mirror". It goes this way:

I'm starting with the man in the mirror
I'm asking him to change his ways
And no message could have been any clearer
If you wanna make the world a better place
(If you wanna make the world a better place)
Take a look at yourself, and then make a change

If you're like most, when you have an issue with someone, you focus on what they did wrong and hope they change so things can get better. Jesus had a different assessment. Jackson got it right too. Change in your relationships starts with the person in the mirror. It begins by taking the log out of your own eyes so you can see well to take the speck out of your brother's. This is the Law of the Log.

As I meditate on this statement of Jesus, a few things begin to emerge. Follow me as we unpack them.

The Five Dysfunctions of the Seer

We See What We Shouldn't See

Jesus said, "Why do you see the speck that is in your brother's eye?" A speck is so small that it is almost impossible to see. This implies, as I heard a preacher once say, that we use a microscope when it comes to the other person's fault. We magnify the faults of others, while we minimize our own. We judge others by their actions while we absolve ourselves from all blame by pointing at our intentions.

We Do Not See What We Should See

Jesus continues, "Why... do (you) not notice the log that is in your own eye?" A log is much bigger than a speck, so it should very visible. Yet we do not see it. Why do we find it easy to find fault in others and find few or none in ourselves? Why are we blind to our own foibles and follies? Interestingly, both the speck and the log are from the same root greek word, implying they are the same substance but different sizes. So what we see in others is actually what exists in us in a bigger measure. It has been said that this is because the lens through which we look at the world is our own self. It is the point of reference we use in judging everyone else. It takes a lot of introspection or humility to see how we are perceived by others and what is wrong with us.

We Say What We Shouldn't Say

The Master continues, "How can you say to your brother, 'Let me take the speck out of your eye,' when there is the log in your own eye?" How can we say the things we say? Talk to any couple in conflict and you will hear the same thing from each partner. The husband says, "She's at fault. She doesn't know how to respect a man." The wife says, "He's the one in the wrong, He doesn't care about anyone but himself." We pontificate profusely about the faults of our brothers and sisters.

We Attempt To Do What We Can't Do

"How can you say to your brother, 'Let me take the speck out of your eye,' when there is the log in your own eye?" How can we remove a speck when we are blinded by our log? No wonder we cause more problems. In fishing for the tiny speck, in our blindness, we puncture the eye of our brothers and sisters. We do them harm because we are trying to do the impossible.

We Neglect To Do What We Should Do

"You hypocrite, first take the log out of your own eye," Jesus admonished. Our first action should be on ourselves, not the other person. According to the Law of Proactivity which we have discussed, we have direct control over ourselves and our responses alone, not on others. Change ought to start with us, then maybe we can help the other party after. This is what we often neglect.

Removing the Log

Removing the log is easier said than done. This is because one of the hardest things to practice is introspection that leads to self-examination and repentance. The log represents things in your life that block your sight. It will take some digging.

Identifying the Log

This log is one with several branches. No wonder we can't see well. We see men as trees. There is a branch that says we know the other person. We understand their intentions and they are wrong. Another branch says we are better and in the right. We are not the one who needs to change, it is them. Another branch of the log represents our unmet needs in the relationship—the things we want so badly for the others to do or say that we are not getting. Another branch of the log is our desire to control. We want people to conform to our mold. They have to make us happy or there will be war. This is not an exhaustive list, but it is a great place to begin the change of the man in the mirror.

Digging Out the Log

True story, but I paraphrase. A woman went to meet a preacher about her wayward son. She complained, "My son doesn't want to go to church anymore. He sometimes doesn't come home at night. He has started drinking and womanizing. My son is lost. Please help me." The wise preacher looked at her and discerned the problem. He said. "You are responsible for what is happening to your son. All these years you criticized him when he made the simplest mistake. You nagged him about going to church, surrounded him with fear and constant censure. You have never praised or appreciated him. Now you are reaping the seeds you sowed."

She burst out crying, agreeing with what the preacher said. "What do I do now?" she asked, sobbing. The preacher answered. "Go back home and leave him alone. Don't preach to him. Don't criticize him. Just surround him with faith and love. Even if he messes up, just love him." The woman left.

A few months later, she met the preacher and told him what took place. At first the son did not believe what was happening. Soon he began to come home more. Then, on a particular Sunday, he asked to go to church with his mom and there he gave his heart to Christ. The woman said, and this is the lesson of the story, "I have a new son now, but the more important thing is that, *HE HAS A NEW MOTHER.*"

She changed. She removed her log and the speck in her son was removed. This is how the Law of the Log works in relationships.

Focus on yourself. You can't change anyone. They are not within your sphere of control— you are. Change starts with the man in the mirror. I hear Jackson say again,

I'm starting with the man in the mirror
I'm asking him to change his ways
And no message could have been any clearer
If you wanna make the world a better place
(If you wanna make the world a better place)
Take a look at yourself, and then make a change.

CHAPTER

18

THE
LAW
OF
THE ROCK

Trust is the rock upon which all great relationships are built. If trust is broken, there is nothing left to build on.

"There are many who say, "You can trust me!"
But can they be trusted?" (Proverbs 20:6 CEV)

ere's another joke from my random collections from the internet.

A defense attorney was cross-examining a police officer during a felony trial—it went like this:

Q: Officer, did you see my client fleeing the scene?

A: No sir, but I subsequently observed a person matching the description of the offender running several blocks away.

Q: Officer, who provided this description?

A: The officer who responded to the scene.

Q: A fellow officer provided the description of this so-called offender. Do you trust your fellow officers?

A: Yes sir, with my life.

Q: With your life? Let me ask you this then officer —do you have a locker room in the police station —a room where you change your clothes in preparation for your daily duties?

A: Yes sir, we do.

Q: And do you have a locker in that room?

A: Yes sir, I do.

Q: And do you have a lock on your locker?

A: Yes sir.

Q: Now why is it, officer, if you trust your fellow officers with your life, that you find it necessary to lock your locker in a room you share with those officers?

A: You see sir, we share the building with a court complex, and sometimes defense attorneys have been known to walk through that room.

I know you got the joke but if you didn't, you are still smart. I want to talk to you about trust in this chapter and locking or keeping lockers open is a perfect analogy for trusting.

Trust is a firm belief in the ability or reliability of a person or thing. A trusted person is one to which the lockers of your heart are open to. You are assured enough of their character and competence that you have removed the key to the lockers of your heart to the extent you believe in their trustworthiness. Since an open heart is necessary for deep friendships and covenant relationships, the type of which is the subject of this book, without trust, only a superficial and guarded relationship can exist. One that nothing of worth can be built upon. Trust is the rock upon which all great relationships are built.

Why is Trust Important in Relationships?

"Don't let your hearts be troubled. Trust in God, and trust also in me" (John 14:1)

Trust is what empties your heart of concerns about a person or their actions in a relationship. This is why it very important. When your heart is not settled about a person's character, propensity, or reliability, you cannot build a meaningful relationship. However, with trust comes freedom of heart to experience the range of what a relationship offers. Trust is the foundational principle that makes relationships possible. Trust is important because:

1. Healthy Relationships are Built on Safety

There cannot be a healthy relationship if there is a possibility of harm from either party. Trust is what assures of safety.

2. Healthy Relationships are Built on Confidentiality

Vulnerability is very essential in relationships. Without trust that the information shared will not be divulged or misused, there cannot be a healthy relationship.

3. Healthy Relationships are Built on Presence

There cannot be a healthy relationship if there are doubts about either party's commitment to being in the relationship. A belief that either party is either not present emotionally or physically or will leave at any time undermines the relationship. This is very important in relationships with kids. Many children have been scarred for life because of adults to whom they opened their hearts but who left them hanging.

4. Healthy Relationships are Built on Consistency

It is hard to build a healthy relationship with someone who does not demonstrate consistency. Erratic behaviors by either party can doom the relationship. A level of predictability is essential for the proper grounding of relationships.

5. Healthy Relationships are Built on Truth

If there is any hint of deception from either party in a relationship, the foundation of the relationship is in danger.

6. Healthy Relationships are Built on Fidelity

Can words be trusted, promises be relied on, and loyalty assured?

7. Healthy Relationships are Built on Competence

Even if all the other qualities are present, a healthy relationship cannot be built if either party lacks either the physical, mental, or emotional competence required in the relationship. A great example is in relationships between two people with vastly different ages, educational levels, or exposure. A belief in either party that the other is incompetent in these areas threatens the foundation of the relationship.

As you can see, the need for trust permeates many areas of relationship. It is impossible to ignore its importance. Its absence leads to all kinds of pain and trouble in relationships.

Building Trust

Unlike forgiveness, which must be given freely, trust must be earned. From the beginning of a relationship and throughout its life, the earning of trust must be continued. However, since you cannot control what the other person does in a relationship, your responsibility is to focus on your part. Become a trustworthy person. Don't start with the big things. Jesus said "Whoever can be trusted with very little can also be trusted with much, and whoever is dishonest with very little will also be dishonest with much (Luke 16:10 NIV). So, develop trustworthiness in little things and it will be an assurance that you will be trustworthy in big things. Here are some ways you can develop trustworthiness.

1. Be Harmless

"Love does no harm to a neighbor. Therefore love is the fulfillment of the law." (Romans 13:10)

Since one of the aspects of trust is the assurance of safety in a relationship, people trust you more when they do not feel threatened in your presence. This comes as you practice what we discussed in the Law of the Center and The Law of Reciprocity. Let people know you are in the relationship to serve them in love. People trust and move toward someone genuinely committed to their well-being and move away from those who they feel threaten it.

2. Keep Promises

"...But let your 'Yes' be 'Yes,' and your 'No,' 'No.' For whatever is more than these is from the evil one." (Matthew 5:37 NKJV)

To become trustworthy, your words must mean something. A person is only as good as their word. One of the characteristics of a spiritual person according to Psalm 15:4 is "Those who... keep their promises even when it hurts." If your words were a bridge over a river and people had to cross them to get to the other side, will they make it safely or will they fall into the river because the bridge broke while they were on it? This is how serious keeping your word is. It starts with little promises made, keeping appointments, calling when you are late, paying bills on time, and so on. While these things may seem insignificant, they go a long way in building trust.

3. Be Transparent

"Therefore, having put away falsehood, let each one of you speak the truth with his neighbor, for we are members one of another." (Ephesians 4:25 ESV)

Transparency is a way of relating in which you show your true self. That means you expose your inner fears and desires, and you express your real opinions and points of view in discussions. A duplicitous person who presents one side of themselves and hides the other should not be trusted. Lasting trust requires that your real self be made known.

4. Keep Confidence

"A gossip goes around telling secrets, but those who are trustworthy can keep a confidence." (Proverbs 11:13 NLT)

In a close or intimate relationship, secrets are shared, and that places a responsibility on you to keep those secrets for each other. Trust is broken if the information shared somehow makes it out to an external party. Practicing the protection of confidentiality is a way of becoming trustworthy in a relationship.

5. Be Vulnerable

"So always tell each other the wrong things you have done. Then pray for each other. Do this so that God can heal you. Anyone who lives the way God wants can pray, and great things will happen." (James 5:16)

This is related to transparency but it narrows to a specific aspect of openness: revealing your faults, missteps, fears, and doubts. Creating an impression that you are Mr. or Ms. perfect will not grow trust because you are not perfect, and it will show. This is where admitting your wrongs and apologizing when you miss the mark is important. Live your truth. Tell your story.

Apologize when you are wrong. Whoever will not accept your truth is not worthy of your friendship.

6. Be Present

"One who has unreliable friends soon comes to ruin, but there is a friend who sticks closer than a brother." (Proverbs 18:24 NIV)

Being present is practicing being there. Let people know you are there for them no matter the season of life the relationship goes through. You cannot be trustworthy if you disappear when you are needed. Practice presence through regular communication. Be there to rejoice with your friends and to weep with them when needed. Be an available shoulder to lean on for your friends. During Job's trial in the Bible, his wife deserted him, but his friends were present. Even the friends of Jesus, apart from a few, deserted him in his troubles. Don't be fickle. Remember the old saying, "a friend in need is a friend indeed".

7. Be Honest

"Whoever can be trusted with very little can also be trusted with much, and whoever is dishonest with very little will also be dishonest with much." (Luke 16:10 NIV)

Honesty is key to trustworthiness. Once you are caught in one lie, it is harder to believe any of your words going forward. Tell the truth even if it hurts. If you can tell the truth when it hurts, it assures people you will be honest in other situations.

8. Be Consistent

"Many will say they are loyal friends, but who can find one who is truly reliable?" (Proverbs 20:6 NLT)

People want a level of predictability in relationships just as you want to know that when you sit on your favorite chair, it is going to hold up your weight and not crumble up on you. You want to know that your car will start every time you turn on the ignition. Being consistent is having a set of values and principles that people can easily identify you with. Let people know where you stand and what you stand for and then stand there over time. Don't be shaky, shady, or shifty. No one will trust such a person.

9. Grow

"When I was a child, I spoke and thought and reasoned as a child. But when I grew up, I put away childish things." (1 Corinthians 13:11)

A belief in the competence of a person is one of the trust builders in relationships. So improve on your competence. When people see you are growing, their trust in you increases. If you are not growing, you will end up acting in certain ways that will cause people to doubt your capabilities or character and it may shake their trust in you. For example, if you display a character weakness that should not be present at your current level of development or responsibility, it may shake people's trust in you. So, commit to personal growth and make constant, never-ending improvements on yourself. Your improved competence through growth will inspire more trust.

10. Trust God

"Trust in the Lord with all your heart and do not lean on your own understanding. In all your ways acknowledge him, and he will make straight your paths." (Proverbs 3:5-6 ESV)

Finally, trust God in all your relationships. Depend on His grace while you do what you can. Commit your relationships into God's hands. His grace is sufficient and capable of making up for all your weaknesses and turning your failings around as you commit them into His hand. He will teach and guide you on what to do in every situation.

Are They Trustworthy?

So what about the other person? How do you prove their trustworthiness? After you have committed yourself to doing these things we just discussed, the same is what you should expect of your partner or friend.

While trusting is a decision you have to make without any guarantee, and you only have control over your own trustworthiness, use the list as a benchmark to assess your relationships. The other party also has to earn your trust, and practicing the things we discussed is how they make deposits in your bank of trust in them. Trusting is an act of faith and you cannot expect perfection. However, it will save you a lot of wasted time and effort if you know where people are. Give them a chance to gain your trust, but if they keep violating these things, it may be necessary to pull the plug on the relationship. You cannot build without a foundation. The Law of the Rock cannot be broken.

Trusting Again

What if you opened the locker of your heart to someone and they came in and stole things, shattering your trust? This is a possibility in relationships. How do you rebuild trust?

Trust can be very difficult to rebuild after it is broken. It will take forgiveness and time. First, you have to forgive yourself and deal with the self-condemnation that comes because you opened up to the wrong person or made yourself vulnerable. You need your heart healed and God is a specialist in that. He came to heal and restore broken hearts.

"The Spirit of the Lord GOD is upon me, because the LORD has anointed me to bring good news to the poor; he has sent me to bind up the brokenhearted." (Isaiah 61:1)

So start by forgiving yourself and the person who broke your trust. Release them. Forgiveness has healing abilities. It flushes the destructive contents left by the betrayal out of your heart and allows you to make room for God's restoration. This is because the natural tendency after your trust has been broken is to close up your heart and never trust again, which would be counter-productive. You must continue living your life.

In starting over, you have to remind yourself again that there still aren't any guarantees. Trusting is an act of faith. Protect yourself by knowing you are capable of working through any hurt that may arise from trusting people. Don't trust less, trust more. The locker of your heart was not made to be locked.

CHAPTER

19

THE
LAW
OF
EXPECTATIONS

Believing the best of people brings out the best in people or at least it keeps you sane. Trust people until they give you enough reasons no to. Even then, find an excuse for them if you can.

"Love bears up under anything, and everything that comes is ever ready to believe the best of every person, its hopes are fadeless under all circumstances, and it endures everything [without weakening]." (1 Corinthians 13:7 AMP)

In 1964 Robert Rosenthal, a Harvard professor performed an experiment in a California elementary school. He wanted to observe what would happen if teachers were informed that certain kids in their class were a group of chosen intellectual bloomers who were expected to succeed. At the beginning of the study, every student in the school took an IQ test. The scores of this test were kept from the teacher. The teachers were then told that some of their students were expected to do very well based on the test. They were then given the names of these expected-to-succeed students. In reality, these students were just selected randomly from the school population.

At the conclusion of the study, all students in the school were then tested again with the same IQ test used earlier at the beginning of the study. It was found that the select group of students, especially those in the younger grades, all showed gains in their IQs. Rosenthal concluded that the expectations of the teachers affected their achievements. This phenomenon of increased performance based on the higher expectations of leaders is now called Rosenthal effect. I call it the Law of Expectations.

Called by a Different Name

"The way you see people is the way you treat them; and, the way you treat them is what they become." - Goethe

Have you ever wondered why Jesus changed the names of some of his disciples? When Jesus met Peter, he was Simon, which means a shaky reed. Jesus named him Peter, which means "rock". I believe this change of name was a demonstration of faith in Peter, despite his shaky nature. Jesus applied the law of expectations regarding Peter's purpose and role in the future church.

I believe this was the motivation behind all the other name changes by God in the Bible: Abram to Abraham, Sarai to Sarah, Jacob to Israel, and others. God released his expectations regarding the futures of these individuals and their lives rose up to His expectations.

Sometimes We All Need Cheerleaders

"When we get together, I want to encourage you in your faith, but I also want to be encouraged by yours." (Romans 1:12 NLT)

A child was trapped in the fourth story of a burning house. The child came to the window and began to cry out for help as the flames engulfed the building. A fireman got on the fire escape ladder to climb to where the child was to rescue the child. As he climbed, the winds blew the flames to make it unbearably hot and dangerous to keep climbing. He hesitated and thought of retreating from this dangerous mission.

Down below, a crowd of people had gathered. As they saw the fireman hesitating, their hearts melted at the thought of the child perishing in the fire if the fireman couldn't reach him. Then someone in the crowd began to cheer. Soon everyone in the crowd began cheering on the fireman. As cheer after cheer went up, the fireman suddenly gathered up courage, climbed through the dangerous fire, was engulfed in smoke, and got the child down to safety. In a situation that could have turned disastrous, cheers made a difference.

Sometimes life can seem like climbing a fire escape ladder while the house is burning. You have a worthy goal but the way up there is treacherous. So you hesitate and may even get discouraged to the point of despair. At such times when you are really tempted to quit and pack it all up, a little cheer can make a whole lot of difference. There is something about well-timed encouragement from someone who believes in you that can suddenly put the springs back to your steps and rearrange the stars that have fallen of your sky. A cheer can put you back in the game of life.

Even Strong People Need The Affirmation of Others

No matter how self-motivated and independent you are, you will need the affirmation of others sometimes. Even Jesus, at the Garden of Gethsemane, needed his friends to stand with him at His darkest hour of trials. Paul shows us the fountain from which such encouragement of faith flows in the words: "When we get together..." Mutual encouragement takes place in fellowship with others. A great company of faith-filled friends who express positive expectations of us is a necessity in life.

Think of the following. Is it possible that the four Hebrew children thrown in the fiery furnace found it easier to stand their ground because they were four not just one? Would Esther have been able to confront the king had it not been for the encouragement of Mordecai? Peter and John went to their company after they had been beaten for preaching the gospel. They joined hands to pray and everyone was cheered. Paul was despondent almost to the point of death until Titus arrived to cheer him up. How about the paralyzed man whose friends broke the roof down to get him to Jesus?

On and on we could go to demonstrate the power of believing the best of people. As iron sharpens iron, so a friend sharpens a friend (Proverbs 27:17 NLT). You need a cheering company too. You need to get together often with such friends. At your most discouraging times, you are tempted to stay away from others, but non-fellowship is like a poison that kills so slowly you may not realize it. An animal out of the pack is easy prey for predators. Sometimes, it is strife and bitterness that keeps you isolated. Guard against that; bitterness makes your circle smaller and smaller until it be becomes a circle of one— you. That's dangerous. Find a company if you do not have one yet. If you do already, utilize it. Get together often, even if it requires effort. Stay in touch with your company. Be a believer in others, and when it's your turn, receive your own cheers gratefully.

Believing the Best

Love believes the best of people. Whatever your role in a relationship, whether you are a parent, spouse, teacher, leader, follower, or friend, it is important to believe the best of the people around you. Your expectations of them surrounds them with faith, which works on their behalf. Express confidence in people. Communicate your great expectations to them. They will start adjusting their actions to match your faith in them and it will become a self-fulfilling prophecy.

This is how to work the Law of Expectations.

CHAPTER

20

THE
LAW
OF
THE COVER

Faulty relationships do not have to be dysfunctional.
Relationships that will work should not give attention to every fault,
but let love cover many faults.

"Above all, keep loving one another earnestly, since
love covers a multitude of sins." (1 Peter 4:8 ESV)

There are several bad cover-ups in history: Watergate, The Ford Pinto Saga, The Dreyfus Affair, the tobacco industry's denial of the health danger of smoking, and The Tuskegee Syphilis Experiment, to name a few. Take the last one. From 1932 to 1972, the "Tuskegee Study of Untreated Syphilis in the Negro Male" was conducted by the U.S.

Public Health Service (PHS) in conjunction with the Tuskegee Institute. Six hundred men were recruited and lied to that they were receiving free medical treatment for "bad blood". However, the real intent was to use them as test subjects and document how syphilis destroyed their bodies over years. Over a 100 of these men died, including people they infected because they were not told they had the disease. Even when penicillin was available in 1947, these men were not offered.

A Cover-up With Lies

In 1960, a government worker saw the report of the study. He first went to the bosses to express his dismay. They did nothing. He then went to the Associated Press with the proof. As the news became public, the study was forced to shut down. That is a textbook example of an evil cover-up. Whenever corporate bodies, government entities, or an individual that sins try to cover-up their sins with lies, it is a bad cover-up and it must be exposed. However, not all cover-ups are evil. When Peter used the word "cover" in the opening text, he uses it in the sense of hiding the sins and faults of others in love.

A Cover-Up With Love

Neither you nor the people in your relationships are perfect. Even when you all mean well, mistakes still happen. There will be faults. They will do things that offend you and you will do the same. If all the faults and mistakes that occur in relationships are given attention, pointed out, and exposed, no relationship will survive. A critical, judgmental spirit will takeover and you will spend most of the time tearing one another down. Soon, what is going on privately within the relationship will spill over to the public as the faults are repeated to others, further driving you apart.

Obeying the The Law of the Cover works to keep this from happening. You accept that your relationships will have faults.

Mistakes, sin, and other failings do not make a relationship dysfunctional. They reveal its humanity and present opportunities to practice and grow in true love and character as you choose to cover multitude of transgressions.

Covering with Forgiveness

"Then Peter came to him and asked, "Lord, how often should I forgive someone who sins against me? Seven times?" "No, not seven times," Jesus replied, "but seventy times seven!" (Matthew 18:21-22 NLT)

Although 70 X 7 – 490 times – is a lot of times to forgive a person, Jesus isn't telling us to forgive our brothers 490 times, he is telling us to *always* forgive them. He follows this statement with a parable about a king who found out his servant owed him the equivalent of millions of dollars. When he asked the servant to pay up and he couldn't, he ordered him and his family to be sold. The servant begged for patience. The king looked at him with pity and forgave all the debt.

The servant then left the presence of the king and found a fellow servant who owed him the equivalent of a few thousand dollars asking him to pay up. The fellow servant pleaded exactly as this servant did with the king but he refused to show mercy, ordering the man who owed him and his family to be sold. When the king heard this from other fellow servants, he was angry, and he had this unforgiving servant delivered to prison until he had paid the debt. Jesus concluded by saying that this is what the Father will do to those who don't forgive people who offended them from their hearts.

If God Treated You the Way You Treat Others

If God treats your faults the way you treat the fault of others, would you survive? Imagine God mentioning your every fault and mistake and asking you to account for them in your relationship with Him. Imagine Him going to other people and telling them your secret sins. Imagine Him withholding forgiveness from you when you ask for it because He wants you to pay for your errors. That would be terrible, wouldn't it?

God treats us with grace. He covers up for us. He forgives us. He does not keep a record of our wrongs. He doesn't treat us as our sins deserve, but He acts towards us with mercy. He practices The Law of the Cover with us. No wonder we love Him.

Increasing Love in a Relationship

"I tell you, her sins—and they are many—have been forgiven, so she has shown me much love. But a person who is forgiven little shows only little love." (Luke 7:47 NLT)

This is a mystery. Jesus was saying the more cover of forgiveness shown toward a person, the more their capacity to love increases. The more forgiveness we retain, the less the capacity to love. If you want your relationships to increase in love, begin to practice The Law of the Cover through forgiveness. Cut the faultfinding and holding on to offense.

Practicing The Law of the Cover in Relationships

Here are some practical ways of applying this law.

Cover to Protect

"Hatred stirs up conflict, but love covers over all wrongs." (Proverbs 10:12)

A hen is a very mild bird until it lays egg or hatches its chicks. Then it turns into a ferocious creature. I remember those childhood days when we would deliberately provoke a mother hen. The first thing it would do was to gather her chicks underneath her wings, covering them, then it would assume an attacking posture ready to pounce on anyone who dared come close to her or put her chicks in danger.

You should realize that offense and faultfinding come into relationships to steal, kill, and destroy. It wants to suck the life out of them and eventually tear them apart. He hates partnerships and what it does for God's plans. You need to become protective like the hen. Fight for your relationships. Resist these evils.

Cover with Forgiveness

"Be kind to one another, tenderhearted, forgiving one another, as God in Christ forgave you." (Ephesians 4:32)

We have already talked about forgiveness. I would like to add the concept of advance forgiveness. Accept that people are going to offend you, then decide in advance that they are forgiven. This is very powerful and liberating. Forgiveness moves from what you do when you are offended but becomes your permanent posture.

Cover with Forbearance

"Always be humble and gentle. Be patient with each other, making allowance for each other's faults because of your love." (Ephesians 4:2)

Forbearance is restraining to enforce a right that is due to you. It is making allowance for faults. You know you have been wronged, but you choose to overlook it as an act of mercy to the offender. This is another way we practice covering multitudes of sin in love.

Cover with Confidentiality

"Whoever covers an offense seeks love, but he who repeats a matter separates close friends." (Proverbs 17:19)

None of us wants our mistakes repeated to others or made public. You will destroy a relationship if you expose the faults of your partner. Keep it within the bounds of your relationship.

Cover with Confession

"Confess your faults one to another, and pray one for another, that ye may be healed..." (James 5:16 KJV)

Practice sharing your own faults and asking for forgiveness. There is something about vulnerability that causes others to act in kind. As both parties admit their faults, the relationship experiences healing.

Cover with Counsel

"Plans fail for lack of counsel, but with many advisers they succeed." (Proverbs 15:22)

Now, there are some faults you may be dealing with in a relationship that you know cannot be handled by both of you. For example, if a spouse has a habit that is destroying the relationship such as abuse, drinking, pornography, and more. Covering, in this case, may require wise exposure. While you will still not go out and broadcast this openly, you can cover this sin by seeking out godly counselors who can help and still provide the confidentiality needed for restoration and healing to take place. Sometimes some sin needs broader exposure for healing to occur. Let this be done with proper guidance

Cover with Forgetting

"Love is patient, love is kind... it keeps no record of wrongs." (1 Corinthians13:4)

Finally, you practice covering with love by forgetting the wrongs of the past. You don't want to keep bringing up past mistakes and faults in relationships. This may be difficult but God's grace is sufficient. Remember what God did for you.

"He has removed our sins as far from us as the east is from the west. The LORD is like a father to his children, tender and compassionate to those who fear him. For he knows how weak we are; he remembers we are only dust." (Psalm 103:12-14 NLT)

Let me end with this story.

A woman met a minister and told him she had been seeing visions of the Lord. The minister wanted to ascertain it was actually the Lord she was seeing. So, he told the woman, "The next time you see the vision, ask the Lord to name one sin I have committed."

The woman went and came back after she saw another vision. The minister asked her what sin the Lord revealed to her.

She replied, "When I asked him about your sin. He simply shrugged his shoulder and said, 'I don't remember.'"

The minister responded to her, "You have truly seen the Lord."

Hallelujah! God has forgotten our sins. Let's extend the same to our fellow brothers and sisters.

CHAPTER

21

THE
LAW
OF
THE FENCE

Relationships need boundaries to thrive. Establish them. Make war to make peace. Confront unresolved issues within yourself and in your relationships with the aim of achieving harmony, then move on.

"If possible, so far as it depends on you,
live peaceably with all." (Romans 12:18)

"Blessed are the peacemakers, for they
will be called children of God." (Matthew 5:9)

I preached a series a couple of months ago entitled "Fences". It focused on addressing several issues that crop up in relationships to fence them from achieving their full potentials. As we come to the end of this book, I would like to share a few of the main points of this sermon series to explain how The Law of the Fences works.

Fences are barriers surrounding a piece of ground for the purpose of marking a boundary, controlling access, or vetting who leaves the grounds. Fences are either protective or restrictive. Physical fences are made up of different kinds of materials: wood, metal, even electronics.

Fences in Relationships

Fences also exist in relationships but they are made of intangibles. They are internal barriers that fulfill the same purposes as physical fences— to either protect or restrict. How you handle the intangible fences in relationships will determine whether you are protected or restricted. Here are some ways they play out in relationships.

1. On the Fence

"Elijah challenged the people: "How long are you going to sit on the fence? If God is the real God, follow him; if it's Baal, follow him. Make up your minds!" Nobody said a word; nobody made a move." (I Kings 18:21 MSG)

Being on the fence is also called fence-sitting. A fence-sitter is someone who remains neutral or undecided in a situation. They are undecided and uncommitted to a side of the issue. They waver between options and end up not standing for anything or doing a little bit of everything.

In relationships, those who sit on the fence are those who are afraid to engage. They are wary of relationships especially deep ones, so they end up missing out on the amazing benefits relationships adds to life and destiny. This may be because of past hurts or observed failures in other relationships.

I have met people who are reluctant to get married because

they have seen so many failures in the marriages around them. Others don't feel they can trust anyone again because their trust has been broken so many times in the past. Disappointments and deferred hope has closed their hearts.

"Hope deferred makes the heart sick; but when dreams come true at last, there is life and joy." (Proverbs 13:12 TLB)

"I don't mean to say that I have already achieved these things or that I have already reached perfection. But I press on to possess that perfection for which Christ Jesus first possessed me. No, dear brothers and sisters, I have not achieved it, but I focus on this one thing: Forgetting the past and looking forward to what lies ahead, I press on to reach the end of the race and receive the heavenly prize for which God, through Christ Jesus, is calling us." (Phillipians 3:12-14 NLT)

Paul touches on several reasons why people sit on the fence instead of diving into life.

a. Fence-sitters Sit on Their Past
They can't forget it

b. Fence-sitters Sit on their Present
They think it is all there is

c. Fence-sitters Sit on Their Future
They've stopped reaching for it

d. Fence-sitters Sit on their Shortcomings
They think this is all they can be

It is dangerous to be a fence-sitter. You stay stuck. You need to get off the fence. Dive back into life. Make peace with yourself by making war on your fears and insecurities. Dare to love again. Dare to trust again.

2. Offense

"Then Satan entered Judas, called Iscariot, one of the Twelve. And Judas went to the chief priests and the officers of the temple guard and discussed with them how he might betray Jesus. They were delighted and agreed to give him money. He consented, and watched for an opportunity to hand Jesus over to them when no crowd was present." (Luke 22:3-6 NIV)

Chicago has been named the rattiest city in the United States followed by New York, Washington DC, Los Angeles, and the Bay area of California. These are the cities where a lot of people are in the rat race but are literally losing the rat race. In Chicago, the north side is the most notorious.

To deal with rats, you have various methods at your disposal. The crudest is to run after them with a stick or try to stamp them out with your boot. It works if you are as fast as them. A more effective method is to cut of its food source by keeping garbage inside heavy duty trash bags and in bins with lids. If the rat can't eat, it will either die or go elsewhere. This is very effective but not always practical because there are many food sources around and people really don't take care of trash well. Another method is to identify the pathways these rats use and then block them with proper "fencing". Another method is to use rodenticides and place them in rat burrows and pathways so they eat or come in contact with them and die. The most effective method is to use traps that have been baited in order to catch these rats and eliminate them.

"Again I say, don't get involved in foolish, ignorant arguments that only start fights. A servant of the Lord must not quarrel but must be kind to everyone, be able to teach, and be patient with difficult people. Gently instruct those who oppose the truth. Perhaps God will change those people's hearts, and they will learn the truth. Then they will come to their senses and escape from the devil's trap. For they have been held captive by him to do whatever he wants." (2 Timothy 2:23-26 NLT)

The second type of fencing activity in relationships are offenses. Offenses are the bait of Satan to trap you. It is a restrictive fence. Paul warned Timothy as a servant of God not to fall into the trap. Judas fell into this trap and it ended his life. The greek word *skandalon*, used for offense in the Bible, means "a stick for bait (of a trap), generally a snare, a stumbling block, an offense. It is something that trips you up into a trap." So the real biblical definition of offense is an insult or action with the capability to trip you up and cause you to fall into Satan's trap. It is a poison that, when it takes root within a person, begins to cause all kinds of trouble and then spread to others to create further destruction.

"Look after each other so that none of you fails to receive the grace of God. Watch out that no poisonous root of bitterness grows up to trouble you, corrupting many." (Hebrews 12:15)

In his book, *The Bait of Satan*, John Bevere explained that offenses are usually sparked by a sense of betrayal. It may start by hearing that someone said something to you or about you that hurt or they took something that belongs to you fraudulently. The sense of betrayal can take root and turn into offense if you are not careful. If you take this bait from Satan, the damages will start within you and in your relationships, and continue extending. They can be huge and costly.

The next fence in relationships expounds on how to deal with offenses when the come.

3. Defence

So how do you deal with offenses in order not to take the bait and get trapped? This I call defense. First, there is a wrong way.

"A brother offended is harder to win than a strong city, and contentions are like the bars of a castle." (Proverbs 18:19)

The wrong approach involves withdrawing and isolating yourself. The person who takes the bait of the offense is the one who ends up imprisoned in bars of isolation. Offense becomes a fence around them that bars them from making further progress in their callings in life because they can no longer forge the manful relationships it requires.

The right defense against offense is what is called peacemaking. It is climbing the fence by confronting conflicts in relationships with love, making war on conflict in order to make peace. The following steps using the acrostic GO CLIMB will help you overcome offense.

How To GO CLIMB Of-FENCE

G- God is the fair judge. First entrust all to him.

"For God called you to do good, even if it means suffering, just as Christ suffered for you. He is your example, and you must follow in his steps. He never sinned, nor ever deceived anyone. He did not retaliate when he was insulted, nor threaten revenge when he suffered. He left his case in the hands of God, who always judges fairly." (1 Peter 2:21-23)

O- Overcome evil with good: Decide to pay forward what God has done for you.

"Do not be overcome by evil, but overcome evil with good." (Romans 12:21)

C- Check your Conscience and Confess your own fault to Clear it. Even if you feel you are right, confess that you may be wrong and seeing things from your own perspective. Vulnerability is the key to disarming offense.

"This being so, I myself always strive to have a conscience without offense toward God and men." (Acts 24:16 NKJV)

L- Look. See the real person behind the offense (Satan) and consider the purpose, not the person that offended you.

"For we are not fighting against flesh-and-blood enemies, but against evil rulers and authorities of the unseen world, against mighty powers in this dark world, and against evil spirits in the heavenly places." (Ephesians 6:12 NLT)

I- Initiate conversation with that person alone first.

"If another believer sins against you, go privately and point out the offense. If the other person listens and confesses it, you have won that person back." (Matthew 18:15 NLT)

M- Mute Maturity. Do not repeat the offense to other people. Offense has a way of resurrecting and perpetuating through repetition.

"Above all, love each other deeply, because love covers over a multitude of sins." (1 Peter 4:8)

B- Be willing to accept the outcome even if it means being cheated.s

"Joseph said to them..."But as for you, you meant evil against me; but God meant it for good." (Genesis 50:19–20)

"The very fact that you have lawsuits among you means you have been completely defeated already. Why not rather be wronged? Why not rather be cheated?" (1 Corinthians 6:7)

If you practice these, you will always through God's grace, overcome offense.

4. No-Fence

The final fence issue in relationships we will discuss is the establishment of proper boundaries. All relationships require boundaries. Boundaries are guidelines or limits that define your interactions with others based on your values. Some believe that all boundaries are restrictive, so they advocate for a no-fence approach to relationships. They say we can all do whatever we like as long as love is present. That would be good if true love is understood. True love has boundaries and they can sometimes be strict. There is also something called tough love. People who establish no fences in their relationships make it vulnerable to detrimental forces coming from within or outside the relationship. The following are some examples of boundaries that may be necessary in your relationships.

The Boundary of Space

"When you're given a box of candy, don't gulp it all down; eat too much chocolate and you'll make yourself sick; And when you find a friend, don't outwear your welcome; show up at all hours and he'll soon get fed up." (Proverbs 25:16-17 MSG)

No matter how intimate a relationship may be, people still need breathing space. It is important to know when to step back and allow your friends have time to themselves. You may kill the relationship if you do not respect this boundary and continually demand they be with you or do things with you. You should know when to step back and let them be. There are times they don't want to be called or disturbed. Even married couples should have their me-time when they can commune within themselves and with God.

The Boundary of Standards

"Don't cheat your neighbor by moving the ancient boundary markers set up by previous generations." (Proverbs 22:24 NLT)

It is said that if you stand for nothing, you will fall for anything.

There are required standards for every type of relationships. There are standards for single people in relationships, for example in the sexual arena. There are standards of how married people and singles of the opposite sex should relate. There are standards of how married friends of the opposite sex should conduct themselves. Leaders have standards. There are rules of follower-ship. Establishing the appropriate boundaries and standards in all your relationships will protect them from destructive forces.

The Boundary of Strangers

"Drink water from your own well— share your love only with your wife.16 Why spill the water of your springs in the streets, having sex with just anyone?17 You should reserve it for yourselves. Never share it with strangers." (Proverbs 5:15-17 NLT)

Sometimes, two is a company and three is a crowd. There are relationships, such as the relationship between spouses, that require a level of exclusivity to succeed. When the original marriage was instituted, it was said that a man would leave his father and mother and cling to his wife. When these boundary is violated, crushing external forces affect the relationship afterward. Engaged or courting singles also need a measure of exclusivity. You can't continue dealing with the opposite sex as you used to do before getting into a serious relationship. If you do, you will open your relationship to problems.

The Boundary of Separation

"Don't team up with those who are unbelievers...Therefore, come out from among unbelievers, and separate yourselves from them, says the Lord. Don't touch their filthy things, and I will welcome you" (2 Corinthians 16:14,17 NLT)

Sometimes relationships have to be terminated because they are not working, have become detrimental to the parties involved, their seasons are over, or they are in disobedience to God. Except for certain covenant relationships like marriage, which have stringent standards guiding their dissolution, every other relationship should make room for the possibility of termination. Don't stay in a relationship that you know violates God's word, your conscience and values. Don't stay in a relationship that drains and dis-empowers you. Even God-ordained relationships can reach their expiry dates. It is important to establish this boundary.

Keeping the The Law of the Fences will add the necessary protective layer to your relationships and your great destiny.

In Conclusion

Thank you for reading until the end. It was a joy to write this book. I felt the love of God coursing through me as I wrote and I hope that as you read, you felt the same. I know it is a lot to digest but I present this as seeds you can pick up at any time to meditate on and then use to breathe fresh life into your relationships.

Please know you are precious to God. He loves you and wants the best for you. He wants you to experience his love and spread it to all that you are fortunate to meet in life. May God's grace and peace continue to abound in your life. Feel free to write me if you'd like to. I will be glad to hear from you.

I would like to end with this with a poem I wrote celebrating God's love over 25 years ago. It is old but its message is always fresh. Enjoy!

Love is not eyeing a dame
It is not a dangerous game
Love isn't the vent of emotions
Not lust set in motion

Love is no intoxicant
Not a feeling to recant
Love isn't blind
Not a child of the mind

Love isn't a bug that bites
It isn't a wedding rite
It's not the rage of desire
No passion's untamed fire

Love isn't a date
It isn't hooking up with a mate
It's not a pit into which you fall
Or a romantic gift from the mall

And Love isn't even a passionate kiss
So, let me tell you what it is
Love is God, in you, on you,
Expressed through you, in all you say and do.

I love you!

MEET THE GREATEST PERSON ALIVE!

I want to share with you about the most important decision that you can ever make in life. Jesus came to the earth to live and die, so that you might have life and live life abundantly, but the devil also has come to steal, kill and destroy. Winning or losing in life depends on whose lordship you are under; either Jesus or the devil. Romans 10:9 says that if you confess Jesus as Lord with your mouth and believe in your heart that God raised Him from the dead, you will be saved. You can yield your life over to the Lord Jesus Christ by saying this simple prayer:

Lord Jesus, I acknowledge that I'm a sinner. I believe that you came to the earth to die for my sins and you rose from the dead to give me life abundantly. I confess you as Lord of my life. I ask you to come into my heart and make me a brand new person. Amen.

If you just prayed this prayer and you meant it, Jesus has come into your life and has made you a brand new person. He has delivered you from the authority of the devil, and has given you dynamic power to live life abundantly. We will like to know of your decision, so that we can stand with you in prayer, and send you faith-building materials to help you in your walk with God.

Please write us at info@thecitylight.org or call our number toll -free: 1-888-LIGHT-21.

To order more copies of this book or other inspiring books,
visit:
www.pastorlan.com
Also available at www.amazon.com

More Books by the Author

Just Before You Say I Do: A Roadmap for Singles

Mission Possible: Finding and Fulfilling your Life's Assignment

Irresistible Influence: You Can Also Make a Difference